Play in Practice

▶▶▶▶▶ ▶▶▶▶▶ ▶▶▶▶▶ ▶▶▶▶▶ ▶▶▶▶▶ ▶▶▶▶

Case Studies in Young Children's Play

The Early Childhood Consortium

▶ Bank Street College ▶ Erikson Institute
▶ Pacific Oaks College ▶ Wheelock College

Edited for the consortium by
Cheryl Render Brown and
Catherine Marchant for the
Topics in Early Childhood Education Series

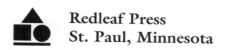
Redleaf Press
St. Paul, Minnesota

Published by: Redleaf Press
A division of Resources for Child Caring
450 N. Syndicate, Suite 5
St. Paul, MN 55104

Visit us online at www.redleafpress.org

Library of Congress Cataloging-in-Publication Data is available.

First, for Nonnie and Poppy, whose unconditional love and devotion to family and one another allowed me the joy of childhood and gave me an intimate knowledge of play before I began to study it. And for Mama, who shared her own vivid memories of play in another time with me.

※

And then, for all the world's children, especially those who know "not enough" only too well. May they know the joys of play, regardless of their race, class, gender, condition, family circumstances, or the politics of their countries. And may their teachers, parents, child life specialists, and social workers be afforded the vision and fortitude to encourage, scaffold, and join them in play.

※

Last and most, I dedicate this book to Len for his love and eternal belief in me, and to Omi, Sash, and 'Miri, who made all that I learned about children and play unfold in the blessing of mothering their ever precious souls. May they always find time to play.

—Cheryl

This book is dedicated to the memory of two former Wheelock colleagues whose lives were cut short this year, but whose spirit and passion live on in those of us who were fortunate to have known them: Susan McBride and Joan Kingson.

—Catherine

Contents

Acknowledgments vii

Introduction ix

Section 1: The Teacher's Role 1

Chapter 1 3
Can Too Many Cooks Spoil the Broth?
Beliefs about the Teacher's Role in Children's Play
Julie Spielberger, Erikson Institute (former), and
Joan Brooks McLane, Erikson Institute

Chapter 2 13
"Teacher, They Won't Let Me Play!"
Strategies for Improving Inappropriate Play Behavior
Vicki Bartolini, Wheelock College, with
Karol Lunn, Wheelock College (former)

Chapter 3 21
Aggression in the Playroom
Teaching Conflict Resolution to Children
Diane E. Levin, Wheelock College

Chapter 4 35
"We Don't Play Like That Here!"
Understanding Aggressive Expressions of Play
Jillian Ardley, Wheelock College (former), and
Lisa Ericson, Wheelock College (former)

Section 2: Cultural Differences 49

Chapter 5 51
What's Wrong with Playing Cowboys and Indians?
Teaching Cultural Diversity to Preschoolers
Amelia Klein, Wheelock College, with commentary by
Carol J. Mills, Wheelock College (former)

Chapter 6 65
"Eenie, Meenie, Mynie Mo"
The Persistence of Racial Definitions in Play
Shirley Malone-Fenner, Wheelock College

Chapter 7 73
"But Are They *Learning* Anything?"
African American Mothers, Their Children, and Play
Kimberly P. Williams, Erikson Institute (former)

Chapter 8 87
The Welcoming Place
Tungasuvvingat Inuit Head Start Program
Gretchen Reynolds, Bank Street College (former)

Section 3: Special Needs and Settings 105

Chapter 9 107
Helping Parents Take the Lead
Preparing Children for Health Care Procedures
Marcia Hartley, Wheelock College

Chapter 10 115
Roundabout We Go
A Playable Moment with a Child with Autism
Amy Phillips, Wheelock College

Chapter 11 123
Eddie Goes to School
Facilitating Play with a Child with Special Needs
Betty Noldon Allen, Tufts University, and
Cheryl Render Brown, Wheelock College

Chapter 12 133
"Every Time They Get Started, We Interrupt Them"
Children with Special Needs at Play
Frances Henderson, Pacific Oaks College (former), and
Elizabeth Jones, Pacific Oaks College

References 147

Contributor Profiles 153

Index 159

Acknowledgments

The editors would like to acknowledge their many colleagues at Wheelock and within the Early Childhood Consortium who supported this project, provided their encouragement, contributed their writings, and supported one another and us in the writing process. Special thanks go to Amelia Klein and Shirley Malone-Fenner, whose unselfish sharing of their knowledge of case-method teaching sparked the idea for this project several years ago.

Our acknowledgments also go to all the students who continue to inspire and teach us about play as they learn in our classrooms and in other settings in the field. They, and the children they care for, teach, and observe, keep us in tune with the need for play.

We also express our deep appreciation to our emeritus faculty colleague, Ed Klugman, who first envisioned the consortium and the potential of faculty collaboration: "You could write about this!" His enduring dedication to play in the lives of children continues to inspire us. We hope that Ed will take justifiable pride in this work, along with each of the authors included in this volume.

We also owe gratitude to Eileen Nelson and others at Redleaf Press for agreeing to be the publishing arm for the consortium's projects. Last, but hardly least, we express deep appreciation to Rose Brandt, who worked diligently with Cheryl to polish the manuscript and advise us on the many details required to bring this book to fruition across the miles from Pasadena to Boston. Without her steady commitment, expertise, and gentle guidance we might never have seen this project through to the end.

This book would have been less without each of their efforts.

Introduction

In spite of great advances in the field of early childhood education over the last ten years, questions rather than answers seem to dominate today's professional conversations about young children and classroom practices. Teaching and learning are such messy and complex businesses that they cannot be reduced to a set of facts, a series of solutions, or a number of guidelines. And just when a question seems to have been answered, other questions arise and beg for investigation. Teaching young children is truly a continual learning process. This book aims to support the lifelong learning of those who work with young children—including, but not limited to, early childhood teachers, child care providers, child life specialists, and early interventionists.

How this book came about

This book is an outgrowth of previous work by the Early Childhood Consortium, a collaborative endeavor of Bank Street College, Erikson Institute, Pacific Oaks College, and Wheelock College. Since 1995, members of the consortium have shared goals and missions including leadership in early childhood education, public policies that support children and families, professional development, and the return of play to its rightful place in children's lives. With the support of Redleaf Press, we have produced a series titled Topics in Early Childhood Education to keep the field informed about our shared efforts.

This book is the third in the series, the natural next step after *Transformational Leadership* (edited by Elizabeth Jones, 1995) and *Playing for Keeps: Supporting Children's Play* (edited by Amy L. Phillips, 1996). The authors in this book, like their counterparts in the earlier books in this series, are affiliated with institutions in the Early Childhood Consortium. Some of the collaborators represented here are colleagues, while others are student-and-teacher pairs. Whatever their relationship, they all share a deep commitment to children's play and to adults' learning about it. This book continues the discussion of the central themes of the earlier books in the series, including adult roles in children's play, multicultural issues related to play, and play in special settings.

Why study cases?

Although it explores the same themes, this book differs from the previous two books in the series in purpose and format. It is meant to be a practice-based companion to *Playing for Keeps*, and therefore focuses more on the sometimes difficult choices inherent in real-life play situations and the way in which we think about those choices. Professional learning is expected to result from reflecting on those choices. While the authors in *Playing for Keeps* described the issues they saw early childhood professionals facing, in this book the authors have created stories, or "cases," based on their classroom experiences to serve as a basis for reflection, discussion, and learning. In developing their chapters, the authors have analyzed their experiences, applied theories to them, and debated their meaning with others. They do not offer solutions to the problems that they have raised, or even try to identify what the real issues might be. Instead, they stimulate their readers to reflect on the material, discuss it, and construct their own knowledge.

The case study method lends itself to the kind of applied reasoning, problem solving, and reflecting that are required of professionals today. Case methodology has become increasingly popular in professional education in many fields, including medicine, business, and human services. The early childhood teacher-education community embraced the use of cases in the 1990s because this approach reflects the messy and complex reality of working with young children. Case studies offer prospective and practicing early childhood professionals the opportunity to apply their knowledge and skills in an integrated and powerful way. As Klein (1996) so aptly puts it, "The case method prepares students to think like professionals" (p. 66). We would add that the case method pushes practicing teachers to think harder as professionals. In our view, cases are the ideal format for deepening our understanding of children's play.

There is a particular place for longer case studies in professional learning because our work with children's play is often based on interactions and relationships over time; the details and nuances build up and become increasingly complicated. Longer narratives can provide an in-depth look at one player, a group of players, a type of play, or an issue relevant to play. They not only describe important incidents but also provide background information that helps the reader understand the participants in the case and the context in which they are operating. They give a complete picture of what is going on and are most effective when dealing with sensitive and complex issues, such as racial bias, cultural misunderstandings, and the play of young children with special needs. For example, chapter 8 shows that we cannot understand the play of Inuit children without understanding their culture, and that a culture cannot be understood without working through the layers of our own beliefs and assumptions. How can we begin to assess what children are learning through play without checking our own assumptions and cultural interpretations? This case forces us to sort out what is really important to us, uncover gaps in our understanding, and come to grips with discrepancies between our beliefs and our actions. Carefully crafted cases and skillfully led discussions can help us discover the "wisdom that can't be told" (Gragg, 1940).

How to use these cases

There are many forms of cases and many ways of using them. For our purposes in this book, cases are "realistic accounts of situations encountered by professionals in the workplace, complete with extraneous information, missing information, and conflicting values of the people involved" (McWilliam, 1992, p. 361). Cases are descriptions of practice, typically written by teachers and teacher-educators, situated in real learning contexts and based on real experiences. They may consist of brief vignettes or extended studies. The cases in this volume range from brief vignettes to fully developed case studies that include multiple scenes and extensive backgrounds. Short or long, they are all raw data that readers can visualize, explore, discuss, analyze, and debate. These cases can furnish discussion material for small groups of practitioners or college students. They aim to generate critical thinking, problem solving, and knowledge construction, for both individuals and groups.

Because these cases are not meant to be easily resolved, they are often emotionally charged and provide ample room for multiple perspectives. They evoke the surprise, anxiety, and other emotional responses that we experience when we fail to accurately predict how events will unfold. For example, chapter 9 leaves the reader uncertain about the "right" way to prepare children for medical procedures. Readers cannot begin to unravel the issues raised by this case without fully understanding the perspectives of the hospital staff helping the family prepare for surgery, the mother, and the child. To evaluate the approach depicted in this incident, readers will need the guidance of a skillful discussion leader who can elicit and help them debate a range of possible responses.

The key to effectively using any of these cases, and particularly the longer case studies, is to choose a focus for reading or discussion. While all the cases are multifaceted and can serve many purposes, we do not advise trying to utilize all that a case may offer in a single reading or discussion. Readers may want to reread a case a second or third time, using the discussion questions as a framework for rereading. Discussion leaders may want to use the questions as a jumping-off point for discussion, or as a guide to working with the case. However they are used, the questions should promote the reader's reasoning about the case material and stimulate a range of possible interpretations.

Finally, cases in and of themselves cannot teach everything that professionals need to know about children's play. Textbooks, research studies, and essays all have a place in furthering our understanding of play. For this reason, many of the authors in this volume have included suggested further resources that they have found useful. By delving into these suggested readings, readers and discussion leaders will gain insight into the case material.

How to get started

This volume isn't intended to be read straight through from cover to cover. It should be a resource that you will pull out whenever a play issue demands further attention and reflection. For example, if you are puzzled by the play of a child with special needs, you might focus on Phillips' case (chapter 10), about a child whose play is less puzzling when considered in light of his diagnosis. If you are struggling with differing perceptions of children's play among the adults with whom you work, you might consider Ardley's case (chapter 4), which shows how adult reactions to play are embedded within the culture of their community.

This book can also function as a source of "discussion starters" for those who are already familiar with concepts about children's play. Spielberger and McLane (chapter 1) and Henderson and Jones (chapter 12) offer rich material for considering how adults grow and change as they find their appropriate places in children's play.

This volume is intended for a broad audience; it is not meant for college use only. It aims to address the common needs of prospective and practicing early childhood care and education providers in public and private settings, as well as family- and center-based programs. It is meant as a medium for enriching the common dialogue among all who work in this field. For example, while Malone-Fenner's case (chapter 6) takes place in a public school, the hurtful racial interactions that it depicts are just as likely to occur in any other setting in which children play. Bias and hatred can take many forms in many places, and all who work with children must address these issues if we hope to prepare children to take their place in a more just society.

However you use them, all of the cases in this book are meant to bridge our ideas about play with actual play experiences and to connect our individual thinking with a more collective understanding. As you read and use these cases, we hope that you will renew your commitment to children's play and will find new insight into your work with children.

How the cases are organized

The authors chose the cases in this book to depict issues about play in a compelling manner. These issues seem to fall into three categories, and we speculate that these categories will be equally compelling to other practitioners. Accordingly, the first section focuses on the role of adults in play, the second on the cultural meanings of play, and the third on issues related to play in special settings. Each section offers a range of opportunities for wrestling with the finer points of the main theme.

The authors in the first section demonstrate how important adults are to children's play, although they offer no formula for the most appropriate way of being involved. In "Can Too Many Cooks Spoil the Broth?" Spielberger and McLane remind us of the ongoing tension between the belief that adults should stay out of children's play and the view that play is and should be a context for learning. In "Teacher, They Won't Let Me Play!" by Bartolini and Lunn and "Aggression in the Playroom" by Levin, the responsibility of adults is further expanded; these chapters show the need for teaching children skills not only for play, but also for life. Finally, in "We Don't Play Like That Here!" by Ardley and Ericson, we see that adults, too, must learn from children's play, if they are to take on effective roles in children's development.

The soul searching deepens in the next section, where we are asked to confront our hidden assumptions about cultural diversity and racial prejudice. In Klein and Mills' "What's Wrong with Playing Cowboys and Indians?" we recognize that play is both embedded in the culture and a medium for learning about it. In Malone-Fenner's powerful "Eenie, Meenie, Mynie Mo," we are reminded of the insidious ways that racial bias can be passed on in play, unless adults intervene. The last two cases in section 2, Williams' "But Are They *Learning* Anything?" and Reynolds' "The Welcoming Place," provide further examples of what play can mean in different cultural groups.

The final section of this book further complexifies play by exploring how special settings and conditions influence children's play. This section shows that play facilitators must understand play from the player's perspective. As Hartley points out in "Helping Parents Take the Lead," the very setting in which the child plays may be inhibiting her play. In "Roundabout We Go," Phillips demonstrates how taking the child's perspective can turn what appears to be disruptive behavior into a constructive play interaction. In "Eddie Goes to School," Allen and Brown show how adults can scaffold a child's activities into play interactions. Henderson and Jones call into question how well our practices actually reflect our intentions in "Every Time They Get Started, We Interrupt Them." Through the play of children in special circumstances, we can gain wisdom about the play of all children.

Section 1

▶▶▶▶▶▶▶▶▶▶▶▶▶▶▶▶▶▶▶▶

The Teacher's Role

Chapter 1

Can Too Many Cooks Spoil the Broth?
Beliefs about the Teacher's Role in Children's Play

Julie Spielberger, Erikson Institute (former), and
Joan Brooks McLane, Erikson Institute

Introduction

When they engage in pretend play, children create imaginary situations—they invent roles and scenarios, and they impose their own ideas and meanings on places, objects, and people. What is the teacher's role in this complex process? On the one hand, play allows children to construct their own knowledge and to act as if they possess various skills and understandings. Some advocates for children's play argue that much of the value of play for children comes from their control of the play situation, from the fact that they are "in charge" of the activity. Other play advocates argue that play is precisely where adults can best assist children in developing new skills and knowledge. Thus, when a teacher enters into children's play, she may be either limiting the expression of their developing competencies, or she may be furthering their cultural knowledge and problem-solving skills.

As indicated in our chapter in *Playing for Keeps: Supporting Children's Play* (McLane, Spielberger, & Klugman, 1996), many factors influence our beliefs about the value of children's play and the teaching practices that deal with children's play in an early childhood setting. Some of these factors are constraints imposed by a particular curriculum or physical setting or the parents' and teachers' goals for children's learning and development, which may be culturally biased. Here we present a brief vignette that describes a pretend-play situation involving a teacher and three children in a child care center. The episode was observed in a classroom in a Title XX child care center serving preschool children from low-income and working-class families. The purpose of this vignette is to illustrate the tension between the idea that play is a domain in which children should be in charge and the idea that play is a context in which adults can facilitate new learning.

Making Play Money

Free-play time, which usually lasts forty-five minutes, has been in progress for nearly half an hour. Three five-year-old children, two girls and a boy, are role-playing in the housekeeping area. They are taking play food out of the cupboard and putting it into a plastic grocery cart. They decide to go shopping, and the two girls put purses on their arms. Then Jarrell tells them, "We need some money." They all go to the adjacent block area, pick up several rectangular blocks to use for pretend money, and put them in the purses and the shopping cart.

The teacher, Ms. Henderson, has been observing their play. She approaches the children and suggests, "Come on over to the table. I'll show you how to make play money." The children follow her to the art table and sit down around her. Ms. Henderson gets out several pieces of paper and a container of markers. She cuts a rectangular shape out of paper and writes the dollar symbol and the numeral "1" in each corner and in the center of the paper. "There, you can make these, too, and then you won't have to use the blocks for money."

All three children become involved in the activity of cutting out pieces of paper and writing numbers and dollar signs on them. Ms. Henderson stays with them at the table for a minute, then she leaves for another area. The children continue to make play money for about five minutes, until Ms. Henderson begins singing a song to signal that it's time to clean up.

Ways to discuss the case

One question that might be asked about this vignette is what difference it makes for children's learning and development to use blocks (the children's choice) as opposed to pieces of paper with the money symbol (the adult's choice) to symbolize real money. The teacher could have chosen to stand back and observe the children's play or to pretend along with the children in using the blocks for money. What was the purpose of her intervention in the children's play, and what did it mean for the children? One point of view is that the children's understanding of money as a medium of exchange was being developed in a playful context, and that the teacher's intervention served to "scaffold" the children to a higher level of realism in representation, as well as to provide practice in number writing.

Alternatively, it could be said that by her actions, the teacher interfered with the children's own construction of knowledge in play. In using the rectangular blocks for money, the children were creating their own symbolic representation. Because it was their creation, the children were solving their "money problem" through a process of collective symbolic representation. In contrast, although the activity of making paper play money extended the children's play ideas, it was initiated by the teacher and did not call upon the children's personal skills in symbolizing or social problem solving. Nor was there any conversation between the teacher and the children about the representational nature of either the blocks or the paper money.

Returning to the question raised above, one critical issue to consider is the extent to which pretend play in and of itself facilitates growth and learning, as opposed to the extent to which pretend play must be socially guided to benefit development. To what extent should adults involve themselves in children's pretend play? What do you believe?

Teachers' beliefs about their role in play

A teacher can assume many roles in children's play (Jones & Reynolds, 1992), and at times these roles can be at odds with one another. We have seen such conflicts between various teacher roles in our observations of teachers and children in Head Start and other preschool settings (McLane et al., 1996). Often these roles have fuzzy boundaries, and a teacher finds herself walking a fine line between facilitating and supporting children's play, on the one hand, and not intruding on and discouraging it, on the other. As a Head Start teacher recently told us, "I think children need to feel bottom-line that play is okay. And that it doesn't mean that because you're an adult, you can't play and it's not important. I think teachers need to know how to play with children, how to step into play, but yet, how to step out of play, and still be an observer within the play." This, she admitted, can be a tricky thing for a teacher to manage.

To help illustrate this further, we will describe the results of part of a research study designed to elicit teachers' beliefs about play in early childhood classrooms (Spielberger, 1999). The vignette described above was part of a written questionnaire that was given to a sample of fifty female African-American Head Start teachers in Chicago. The teachers were asked to read the vignette, and then respond to the open-ended question, "Describe what you see happening here." Their responses not only illuminated what this particular group of women believed about the value of pretend play and the role of the teacher in children's play, but also illustrated the wide range of their beliefs about play.

It should be noted that almost all of the teachers in the sample indicated that they highly valued pretend play for young children in Head Start. However, when responding to the vignette about the children using blocks for play money, they expressed a range of opinions about the role of the teacher in play. While many saw the actions of the teacher, Ms. Henderson, in a positive light, as extending what the children were learning through their play, a majority (64 percent) believed that the teacher was interrupting or interfering with the children's creativity. As you read the opinions expressed by the Head Start teachers, think about how they compare with your own point of view.

The following comments were made by teachers who viewed Ms. Henderson as interfering or taking over the children's play:

"The teacher is not letting the children use their own imagination—they're using hers instead."

"When the teacher, Ms. Henderson, suggested to the children in the house area to make their own money from paper and markers instead of pretending with the blocks, she took away their pretend play. The children had already decided to use the blocks to represent the money."

"The children were using their imaginations and pretending to shop and use blocks as money. They were doing fine; the teacher interrupted their play/work because of her own way and means of doing things, which should not have happened. If a child asked for her help in the situation, it would have been okay to interrupt or join in. Her stopping their way of doing it can cause them to feel inadequate or some other negative way. The children then didn't have time to return to their play."

"I feel that the teacher didn't give the children a chance to act out their play. Had she just observed them longer she might have seen them buying items and pretending the block units were different moneys. When she tried to interact, she turned the activity into something different altogether."

"I think that this teacher was trying to be helpful, but she was out of order. I think that the teacher stopped the children from expressing themselves in their cognitive development. This teacher was not giving the children the ability to think on their own and make their own choices."

The following comments were made by teachers who believed that Ms. Henderson was facilitating the children's play and extending what they were learning:

"I would say that active learning is taking place between the children, with each other, as well as the teacher with children. I feel that as long as there are materials, and children being able to manipulate their environment and language to communicate with each other, there is active learning. Support from adults is important to help them solve their problems and manipulate their environment."

"The teacher showing the children how to make play money is being creative and realistic. Here she is also teaching the children about their shapes and numbers, making their play time fun and interesting. They are also learning to enhance their fine motor skills, along with increasing their cognitive skills."

"Here through play the children are learning and communicating with each other. They are also developing skills such as social and emotional development, cognitive development through role play, language through writing, and classification in investigating and labeling."

"Since Ms. Henderson suggested and didn't tell them they had to make play money, I believe the children enjoyed making play money. The children got involved in cutting and writing, which helped them with their small motor skills. They learned to recognize a rectangular shape, the number 1, and a dollar sign. Since the children didn't have enough time to play with their play money, Ms. Henderson could suggest for them to play on the next day with their play money in the housekeeping area. But I also think it is okay for children to use their own imagination and let them pretend that the blocks represent their play money at times."

In proposing alternatives to Ms. Henderson's actions, several teachers also emphasized that it is important for adults to observe and use children's cues to guide their involvement in children's play. Their comments included the following:

"She should have let them continue in their play, and at small group showed the children how to make money, or she could have pretended along with the children, and become a bank. Therefore she wouldn't have discouraged their play."

"If I were the teacher I would not have interrupted their play. The children were playing socially well and had made the blocks as their money. I thought they were doing great. If the children had asked me if I would show them how to make it, I would have joined the group."

"As a teacher I try not to interrupt children when they have taken on roles during role play. In some cases when an adult interrupts role play, children do not continue their same roles. If this happens the children may not go as deep into the role as they might have. I would have waited until the next day and maybe made this into a math project for the class. The children showed creativity by choosing blocks to put into the cart. And in my opinion creativity should never be interrupted."

"The children have been creative in making their own setting. They are shopping and realize the part money plays in this type of activity, which draws on their real-life experiences. The teacher notices that they are using blocks for money. She believes paper is a better idea or closer replica of money, adding to its realism. Yet, she somehow manages to change a dramatic play activity into a fine-motor art activity. Ms. Henderson was appropriate in mentioning the possible use of paper as money. But her wording might be 'Another way to make money is to use paper.' She demonstrates, leaves, and allows them a choice."

Contextual issues about the teacher's role

Play as an activity can be considered a means or a process in which children "make sense of" and "tell about" the world. According to Vygotsky (1978), the imaginary situation a child creates in pretend play is a necessary *transition* or *zone of proximal development* that assists the child in understanding the link between symbols and the objects and actions they represent. When play is valued as both the "work" and the "natural inclination" of children, it provides opportunities for them to practice, interpret, and internalize language and other representational behaviors that are part of their biological and cultural heritage.

When play is not valued or supported by the physical and social context, its impact on development and learning may be weakened. Pellegrini and Galda (1993) argue that

> adults suppress children's exhibition of competence in symbolic play because when children and adults interact, adults do most of the work, such as initiate interaction and repair breakdowns. In peer contexts, children must negotiate these areas themselves. We stress that these differential adult-child effects are probably specific to the symbolic play context; adults clearly enhance other aspects of children's development. (p. 169)

The opposite position is taken by Schrader (1990) and Morrow (1990) who argue for using symbolic play as a teaching-learning medium for early literacy acquisition. Schrader observed teachers trained in emergent literacy concepts and preschoolers interacting in play centers enriched with literacy materials. She found that children made use of the literacy artifacts in their role-playing activities. Furthermore, when teachers intervened in their play, they were able to redirect them toward reading and writing activities or extend their play. For example, if a child was pretending to go shopping, a teacher might say, "Why don't you write a list of things you need to buy." Or, if a child told a teacher he was writing a letter, she might ask, "Who are you writing to? Did you address the envelope? Will you read your letter to me?" or make suggestions such as "Let's write invitations to a party and mail them."

What should be the adult's—the teacher's—role in supporting and facilitating children's play? As "Making Play Money" suggests, this complex question has no single or simple answer. There may well be a difference between what is learned when children play independently with language, objects, and peers without adult direction, and what is learned when adults intervene in play to facilitate learning. At the same time, there are many factors that impinge on what children and teachers do in early childhood classrooms, such as individual and cultural differences in children and families, the teacher's personal style, the schedule of routines and activities, the teacher's beliefs about how and what children learn, the teacher's goals for children, and what the teacher thinks about the role of play in children's development.

The extent to which play will be valuable for children's learning and development may well depend on how it is perceived and supported by adults. Support for and facilitation of learning through play may come both from opportunities for children to explore and use play materials in their own way and from opportunities to have positive and extended interactions with caring adults. Teachers, in turn, must have the time and opportunity to observe children and their play and to reflect upon their practices in light of their beliefs and goals. This, we hope, will be evident from the reflection and dialogue stimulated by "Making Play Money."

Discussion questions

Use the discussion questions below to guide your observations of teacher-child interactions during free play, and to share and discuss your ideas with other early childhood professionals.

- ▶ How would you describe the activity?
- ▶ Who is in charge of the activity?
- ▶ How would you describe what the teacher is doing?
- ▶ What seem to be the teacher's goals for children's development?
- ▶ What does the teacher seem to believe about the value of play for young children's learning and development?
- ▶ What skills and knowledge do you think children might be developing?
- ▶ What do the children stand to gain or lose from the way that the teacher is involved in their play?
- ▶ If you had been the teacher, what would you have done? Why?
- ▶ How do your own beliefs about play compare with this teacher's?
- ▶ What other information would you like to know to help you interpret this situation?

Here is another vignette that describes an interaction between a teacher and two children in a pretend-play situation. The episode occurred in a preschool room in a university laboratory school serving primarily middle-class children. Read the description and, using the same discussion questions as a guide, discuss your reactions to this episode with your group. How would you compare this teacher's beliefs about the value of play and her role in play with those of the teacher described in the first case? How do her beliefs compare with your own?

The Restaurant

There are twenty-two children, ages three and four years, and three teachers in the room. The morning free play period lasts from 8:30 (arrival time) until about 10:45.

Around 9:15, Sara picks up a play telephone, and with her ear to the receiver, looks across the room at Mrs. Vaughn, the assistant teacher, and calls, "Mrs. Vaughn, I'm calling you." She repeats this a few times before Mrs. Vaughn notices and asks, "Oh, on the telephone?"

"Yes," Sara responds.

"Okay." Mrs. Vaughn picks up another phone. Sara says, "Do you want to come to our restaurant?" Peggy walks over to join the play.

Mrs. Vaughn: "Well, what are you serving?"

Sara: "Peanut butter sandwiches, chicken."

Mrs. Vaughn: "Do you have any soup?"

Sara: "Yes, we have chicken fried soup."

Mrs. Vaughn: "Is that on special?"

Sara: "Yes."

Mrs. Vaughn: "How much does it cost?"

Sara: "It cost $1."

Mrs. Vaughn: "Okay, I'll be over. That's a good deal."

Mrs. Vaughn gets up from the phone, turns, and walks away to another part of the room. Peggy and Sara begin putting dishes out on the table. Peggy calls to Mrs. Vaughn, but she appears not to see or hear her. Peggy goes to her and pulls on her shirt and says, "It's over here, silly, it's over here," pointing to the table in the dramatic play area. Mrs. Vaughn looks over at the table where Sara is setting out dishes and says, "Oh, it's not time to eat yet," and then looks away.

At this point the play seems to dissipate, although ten minutes later Peggy and Sara take a pad of paper and sit with a boy at another table to take his order. A few minutes after that, Mrs. Vaughn does come to the table, sits down with the group, and pretends to drink some tea.

Suggested readings and resources

Bennett, N., Wood, E., & Rogers, S. (1997). *Teaching through play: Teachers' theories and classroom practice*. Buckingham: Open University Press.

Berk, L. E. (1994). Vygotsky's theory: The importance of make-believe play. *Young Children, 50*, 30–39.

Christie, J. F. (Ed.). (1991). *Play and early literacy development.* Albany, NY: State University of New York Press.

McLane, J. B., & Spielberger, J. (1995). *Play in early childhood development and education: Final report to the Spencer Foundation.* Unpublished manuscript.

Roskos, K. A., & Christie, J. F. (Eds.). (2000). *Play and literacy in early childhood: Research from multiple perspectives.* Mahwah, NJ: Lawrence Erlbaum.

Vygotsky, L. (1978). The role of play in development. In M. Cole, V. John-Steiner, S. Scribner, & E. Souberman (Eds.), *Mind in society: The development of higher psychological processes,* pp. 92–104. Cambridge, MA: Harvard University Press.

Wood, E., & Bennett, N. (1998). Teachers' theories of play: Constructivist or social-constructivist? *Early Child Development and Care, 140,* 17–30.

Chapter 2

"Teacher, They Won't Let Me Play!"
Strategies for Improving Inappropriate Play Behavior

Vicki Bartolini, Wheelock College, with
Karol Lunn, Wheelock College (former)

Introduction

The following case study explores the play issues experienced by "Brad," a five-year-old boy in a diverse preschool classroom, as described by Karol Lunn, Brad's early childhood educator. Although Brad is an individual with unique qualities, his case also exemplifies some characteristics that are common to several children Karol and I have worked with over the years as educators in both public and private settings. We chose Brad because we thought that his behaviors were typical of many children and because they seemed to connect with aspects of my previous work, as described in chapter 9 of *Playing for Keeps: Supporting Children's Play* (Bartolini, 1996).

Brad, an only child, attended an inclusive preschool program for three half-day sessions each week. The philosophy of the program embraced play as central to a child's development and child choice as an essential cornerstone of this philosophy. The classroom was designed to provide opportunities for various levels of play (parallel, cooperative, and representational) and various forms of play (blocks, gross and fine motor, literacy, art, music, dramatic play, and so on). The space was well planned and well utilized. The sessions were carefully planned, prepared, and structured to support developmentally appropriate practices and learning.

The Highway Game

"Hi, Karol, what can I do today?" Brad asked, scanning the preschool classroom for inviting play opportunities, like a tiger ready to jump on its prey. He was ignored by the other children who were playing at the block area and the dramatic play area—the play areas that most attracted him. Brad struggled restlessly to make a decision. In the block area, several children were building a highway, with road signs, bridges, tunnels, trucks, equipment, and workers. Sighting this appealing play opportunity, Brad zoomed over and crashed into their ongoing play, accidentally knocking down sections of their carefully constructed highway. "I'll be the truck driver and use the backhoe!" he exclaimed, yanking a toy truck away from another child, making up new rules, and disrupting the play.

"Let's play somewhere else, away from him," said Jamie.

"I'm going to push him back," said Tony. Jamie and Tony moved with the other children to a different play area, leaving Brad alone, puzzled, and hurt.

"They don't like me. They won't let me play with them!" he cried to Karol, angrily kicking over the remains of the highway.

The Fire Emergency

On another morning, Brad eyed the children in the dramatic play area, who were playing "fire station." The children had agreed on their rules for a fire emergency. The chief firefighter, the EMT, and the victims (a "mother" and her "baby") were busily planning a daring rescue. Along came Brad. "I'll save the baby!" he yelled, grabbing the doll away from Louisa. He turned to the others, laughing and jumping up and down with excitement, thinking that he had successfully joined in and that he was sharing in the fun.

Louisa complained. "Karol, make him leave. He's bothering us!"

"No, I'm not!" said Brad. "I can play here, too, if I want to!" Brad did not realize that he had managed to upset everyone in his effort to join in and play with the group.

Karol responds to Brad's situation

Brad hasn't yet acquired the skills needed to successfully join in and adapt to an ongoing play scenario. Therefore, Karol is challenged to defuse both Brad's feelings of frustration and those of the other children, as well as respond to their exclusion of him. Karol tries to help Brad acquire more appropriate social skills by talking with him, modeling appropriate behavior, and helping him gain self-awareness and social perception. The following discussion examines not only Brad's behavior, but also Karol's search for appropriate strategies to assist him.

Karol observed that Brad couldn't understand why the others didn't want to play with him, why they excluded him, or (from his perspective) didn't "like" him. He didn't seem to understand how his own behavior was affecting the goal that he wanted so badly to achieve.

This counterproductive behavior occurred consistently in the dramatic play area, as described in "The Fire Emergency" (see also Bartolini, 1996). Typically, Brad would notice an inviting scene unfolding. In this situation, the other children had already determined their roles, such as chief firefighter or EMT. They had agreed on their responsibilities, such as equipment operation, and they had determined the goals of the play, such as "rescue the baby on the second floor." Brad would come along and dive right in, without any sense of what role he might play, where he might fit in, or what was occurring in the play scenario. He might grab props, such as a fire hose or safety helmet, from another child, without any apparent regard for their rights, disrupting the play with his zeal. "I'll be the fire chief. Let's spray the house!" At this point, the play scenario would dissipate, because the mutual goals and rules were no longer being observed. Typically, the other children would exclude Brad, ask him to leave, complain about him to the teacher, or move to another area.

Each time, Brad would be left disappointed, confused, hurt, and frustrated by his failure to successfully enter and navigate a play situation. He would often turn to one of the teachers, usually Karol, to solve the problem for him. He would ask her to make the other children let him play with them and do it his way—appealing to her to compensate for his lack of appropriate social skills.

Initially, when Brad became frustrated or upset Karol would try to calm him by patting his back or putting her arm around him. However, she soon learned that Brad didn't seem to respond to this approach, although it often has a calming, quieting, and reassuring effect on some children. He seemed to recoil from any physical response, and sometimes he would become even more upset.

Karol then tried to reason with Brad. She tried to help him see how his behavior was disrupting the play. She tried to explain to him that he needed to enter play situations in ways that were acceptable to the other children and negotiate his way into the ongoing play. However, Brad was often so upset and excited that he would not listen. Despite repeated efforts, attempts at explanation seemed to have little or no effect on Brad; he wouldn't stand still and think it through.

Next, Karol had to model how Brad might navigate the play situations differently. When he identified an activity that he wanted to join, she would tell him to watch her, to see how to be accepted into the play scenario. Brad seemed to like this and would watch intently. Karol would play the scenario in both positive and negative ways, and ask Brad what would happen if she grabbed a truck or if she nicely asked for it. After modeling the behavior for him, she would discuss it with him and ask him what he had observed. She would model different ways to enter an ongoing play scenario. She would ask, "Would it be okay if I played with you?" Once accepted, she would demonstrate how to negotiate her role in the play, by asking, "Could I be in the rescue squad?" or "When you're done being the fire chief, could I have a turn?" She looked for opportunities to show Brad how to compromise, negotiate, and express himself appropriately.

Karol also felt that she needed to be very explicit about the consequences of Brad's misbehavior. When he pushed children or grabbed toys, he would be excluded from the play situation; that was the consequence and he understood it. He seemed to need explicit expectations and consequences for inappropriate interactions. For example, if he were accepted into a play sequence, he had to realize that if he didn't compromise he would be excluded from the play, and that Karol would not rescue him. This was difficult for Brad to learn; with no other children at home, he seldom needed to compromise. According to Brad's mom, he could usually scream and get what he wanted.

Finally, Karol tried to help Brad improve his social perception skills, to help him "read" a play situation. She would encourage him to observe what was unfolding in a play scenario to help him accurately assess how he might contribute. Then she would encourage him to consider how he might join in successfully, by asking, "What do you think is happening? Who is doing what (doctor, nurse, chef, teacher, and so on)? What could you say to the other children so they'll let you join?" If Brad looked espe-cially excitable, she would ask, "What would happen if you ran over and pulled the doll away from Louisa?" This approach helped Brad consider the positive and negative consequences of his alternatives. Karol felt that this attempt to improve Brad's social perception skills showed some results, after much practice on both their parts.

Vicki's Perspective

In chapter 9 of *Playing for Keeps*, I discuss the interpersonal or "people skills" described by Daniel Goleman in *Emotional Intelligence* (1995). Goleman describes the qualities that he feels characterize people who excel in life, such as persistence, zeal, self-motivation, empathy, social deftness, self-awareness, and impulse control. I also refer to Howard Gardner's theory of multiple intelligences (also discussed by Goleman), particularly the quality that Gardner refers to as "interpersonal intelli-gence." According to Goleman, interpersonal intelligence is comprised of four kinds of skills: leadership skills, mediation skills, relationship skills, and insight skills. I also discuss Berk's interpretation of Vygotsky's work about the importance of representational play. Berk refers to Vygotsky's discussion of representational play as an opportunity for a child to devel-op social competence, impulse control, delay of gratification, rules of acceptable social behavior, and self-regulatory behavior.

Brad's deficiencies in social perception, interpersonal skills, impulse control, and delay of gratification are important developmental areas that need attention and support, since children must learn these skills by fol-lowing the rules of social behavior during play. Karol modeled appropriate behavior and took advantage of Brad's strong verbal skills to help him learn to enter and adapt to particular play situations. Karol identified a number of issues that she grappled with in her attempts to understand Brad's needs and determine the strategies that she could use to help him.

First, Karol felt that Brad was unable to "read" or "scope out" a situa-tion before attempting to join in—instead, he would simply plunge right in. She also felt that he lacked the social skills to negotiate his way into group play. These issues seemed to be related to deficiencies in impulse control, delay of gratification, and social perception.

Once Brad entered a play situation, he appeared to have difficulty compromising his desires, waiting for his turn, and showing empathy for others in the group. According to both Berk and Goleman, these skills are related to self-regulatory behavior. For example, from Goleman's perspective, Brad would need to replace his impulsive behavior with self-regulatory behavior. Goleman suggests that the control of impulsive behaviors may support the development of empathy, which involves genuine listening to others and the ability to view experiences from another's perspective.

In addition, Brad didn't seem to understand his role in disrupting the play scenario and ultimately being isolated by the other children. This lack of awareness may also be related to the development of empathy and the ability to consider the feelings of others. Perhaps it is related to the egocentrism that is commonly associated with preschool-age children.

It's important to consider Brad's play skills from a developmental perspective; this would include his communication and language skills, social perception skills, interpersonal skills, cognitive development, and impulse control or self-regulatory behavior. In devising her plan to help him, Karol relied on her own knowledge of child development and informal consultations with other educators.

Karol questioned her role as teacher/facilitator in guiding, scaffolding, supporting, and responding to Brad's play behaviors, failures, and frustrations. She wondered if it might be better to let the situation follow its natural course and consequences. She considered the appropriateness of interfering with the play of the other group members in her attempts to assist Brad. She also considered her role in responding to Brad's frustrations, as well as working with the other children who became frustrated with Brad and excluded him.

Through trial and error, Karol found that there were three strategies that seemed most helpful to Brad. First, she modeled appropriate behavior for entering group play, compromising, and negotiating desires. Second, she explained what she was going to do, to focus his observations of her as she modeled the behavior. Finally, she guided him in learning to read a situation before plunging in, having him stop to observe and discuss what steps he might take to achieve his goals.

Brad's case is representative of the issues presented by several children that Karol and I have worked with over many years of teaching. We feel that these issues are particularly important to examine because of their link to the lifelong skills required by adults for success in the workplace and for the establishment of family and social interactions.

The worker of the future is unlikely to have the security of a lifelong position. Rather, most workers of the future will need to consider themselves self-employed and will need to rely on their emotional intelligence and interpersonal skills to respond flexibly to the demands and needs of a rapidly changing workplace. More than ever, adults will need to be able to "play" effectively with others. This skill will involve the ability to read an interpersonal situation; to understand how to compromise and negotiate with others; and to exhibit self-regulatory behaviors, such as impulse control, delay of gratification, and empathy.

Preschool play is "on-the-job training" that offers many wonderful opportunities for young children such as Brad to practice and acquire these important skills. Early childhood educators such as Karol are wise to realize the lifelong importance of these sophisticated play skills, and the importance of the teacher's role in supporting the learning of these skills through play.

Discussion questions

- ▶ What other kinds of information might be important and useful in helping us understand Brad's play issues?
- ▶ What kinds of skills does a child need to successfully join in a play scenario already in progress?
- ▶ Are Brad's difficulties in navigating these play scenarios typical of the developmental issues faced by five-year-old children?
- ▶ What strengths does Brad seem to bring to the play scenarios?
- ▶ Should the teacher intervene, or let the children resolve their play issues alone?
- ▶ If the teacher were to intervene, what should the teacher do?
- ▶ What skills might the teacher focus on to help Brad achieve success in joining in a play scenario in progress?
- ▶ Should the teacher involve anyone else in evaluating this situation?
- ▶ How should the teacher work with the other children?
- ▶ What recommendations might the teacher make to Brad's parents or caregivers?

Suggested readings and resources

National Association for the Education of Young Children. (1991). *Accreditation criteria & procedures.* Washington, DC: Author.

Chapter 3

Aggression in the Playroom
Teaching Conflict Resolution to Children

Diane E. Levin, Wheelock College

Introduction

Chapter 6 in *Playing for Keeps: Supporting Children's Play* (Levin, 1996) describes how the process of play is a central avenue through which children construct knowledge and skill. That article argues that when children fail to engage in creative and personally meaningful play, many aspects of their development and learning can be negatively affected. It also describes many contemporary factors that are undermining play, for instance, poverty, violence, the media, and media-linked toys.

Many children today spend less time playing than children did in the past, and when they do play, their play is often dominated by content from TV, much of which is violent. This produces a more imitative play process than when children bring the full range of content from their experience into their play. When play is dominated by television, adults must play an important role in facilitating a more creative play process.

The three vignettes that follow are designed to help students learn to facilitate play in a key area in which play is often jeopardized—social problem solving and conflict resolution. Each vignette consists of two parts. The first part describes a conflict that arose during play. The second part shows how the teacher responded. The response illustrates how adults can help children learn the kinds of skills they need to work out their own conflicts in ways that help to sustain and even extend their play.

The analysis that follows the vignettes offers a framework for helping students understand why the teachers responded to the children's play conflicts as they did (using an approach that is also adaptable to non-play conflicts). Students can use the open-ended discussion questions to discuss the two phases of each vignette.

Thanks to Rena Arcaro-McPhee for contributing the scenario for "Choosing Superhero Roles." "Medical Play Hits a Hurdle" is adapted from *Teaching Young Children in Violent Times* (Levin, 1994).

Choosing Superhero Roles

Out in the play yard, I found four-year-old Henry crying beneath the tire climber. I didn't have a clue what had happened. I knew that when playing outside, he often runs with a pack of children (mostly boys) who love superhero play. I went over and asked if I could help him, because I could see that he was upset. He sobbed, "I just wanted me to be the White Power Ranger and Jay said I couldn't." I knew that this wasn't the first time that these boys had run into trouble assigning roles for their superhero play.

The Teacher's Response

I comforted Henry about his disappointment and suggested that we bring all the boys who were playing Power Rangers together to discuss the problem. He nodded yes. I called the group over and told them that Henry had been crying and that they needed to hear why.

Henry: "I want to be the White Power Ranger."

Jay: "But we already have one. Ray is the white one!"

Henry: "But I want to play too."

Jay: "But you can't be the White Power Ranger. We already have one. There's only one."

Teacher: "So I hear your problem. Ray and Henry both want to be the White Ranger and there's only supposed to be one."

Ray: "I'm the White Ranger. Jimmy said so."

Teacher: "So Ray is playing the White Power Ranger and Henry feels really bad that he can't be. What do you think you could do so everyone is happy?"

Ray: "Everyone has a part; we have all the Power Rangers already."

Evan: "Maybe he (Henry) could play tomorrow."

Teacher: "How does that sound, Henry?"

Henry: "Not good. I still want to be the White Ranger."

Joel: "I know, why don't we have two White Rangers, Ray and Henry?" At this suggestion, Henry brightens up, and the boys all agree that this is a great idea.

Teacher: "Does that sound okay to everyone?"

All the boys: "Yes!"

Teacher: "Before you start playing, can you tell me a little about what the two White Rangers will do, Jay?"

Clancey: "We never had two of the same Ranger."

Ray: "We better stay together so there's one to do our job."

Teacher: "Ray, do you mean that you and Henry will work together to both do the White Ranger's job?" Ray nods.

Henry: "Yeah. We do all the things together so we're more strong."

Teacher: "Okay. Let's see you give it a try. Let me know how it works."

Learning to Take Turns

A group of three-year-olds are excited about a small trampoline (about 4 inches from the floor) that has just arrived in their classroom. Even though the teacher calls on one child at a time to go on it, she often has to remind the children that they need to "take turns," because they keep trying to climb on during someone else's turn. When the teacher has to turn her back for a moment, several kids get on at once and one child falls off onto his knee and begins to cry.

The Teacher's Response

Teacher (squatting down to comfort the crying child): "Oh, dear. Jackson is crying. It looks like there's a problem taking turns with the trampoline."

Jackson: "I waited; it was my turn."

Angela: "Joelle was on."

Teacher: "It's really hard for all of you to wait so long to have a turn on the trampoline. So many of you want to use it and there's only one trampoline. But when you don't take turns it's not safe; Jackson got hurt."

Jackson: "Joelle stepped on my foot really hard."

Joelle: "I pushed him off. It was my turn."

Teacher: "So when two people get on at once a kid's feet can get hurt. It sounds like we have a problem here. A lot of kids like the new trampoline and want to have a turn. They're having a hard time waiting and kids are getting hurt. How can we use the trampoline so everyone is safe, and no one gets hurt?"

Gretchen: "Take your shoes off."

Teacher: "So you think children should take their shoes off before they get on, so other kids' feet don't get stepped on. Okay, let's have you take off your shoes. Put them here along the wall. I'll make a picture of that idea to help you remember." The teacher draws a simple picture of a shoe with a line through it and a bare foot with no line. "Any other ideas?"

Neila: "Take turns."

Teacher: "How would that work?"

Tai: "Only one at a time."

Teacher: "We tried that. It was really hard. Jackson got hurt. How can you know when it's your turn?"

Kerry (to teacher): "You say whose turn."

Teacher: "I need you to help me. I have an idea—let's make a big circle around the trampoline and then we go around the circle taking turns. Then you'll know whose turn it is."

The children start joining hands to make a circle, the way they do at story time. The teacher makes a picture of the trampoline with one stick-figure person on it and other stick people holding hands around it.

Teacher: "Look at that good circle you've made. Let's have Joelle go first, since her turn got stopped when Jackson got hurt; then Harvey, because he's next to Joelle, then Jai, who's next to Harvey." The teacher goes all around the circle in this way, listing all the children's names in order.

Jeffery: "We should count to five."

Teacher: "You mean we should count as Joelle jumps, so we know when her turn is up?" The children are used to this approach to taking turns from counting a specific number of stirs when cooking. The teacher leads the children in counting to five as Joelle jumps. When they get to five, Joelle whimpers that it's too short. The other children seem to agree.

Teacher: "It sounds like you don't want to use 'five' for turns. Should we try using a bigger number?" The children call out many numbers, ranging from three to a million. The teacher helps them try out some of the numbers. This provides a new focus for the trampoline activity—working out how long a turn should be.

Medical Play Hits a Hurdle

Nathan and Delise are playing hospital in the dramatic play area of their child care center. Delise, who in real life has recently been briefly hospitalized for minor surgery, is playing the patient. She's lying on a bed with "bandages" (torn strips of sheets) wrapped around her head, arms, and legs. She looks as if she's in terrible shape. The doctor, Nathan, is standing over her with a stethoscope.

Nathan puts the stethoscope down and picks up a play syringe, saying, "You're shot. Your heart is bleeding. You need this to get it to stop."

Delise: "No, it's gonna hurt."

Nathan: "Be still. You need it to save your heart. It's bleeding really bad."

Delise (sitting up and pulling off the bandages): "No! You stop that. I'm better."

Nathan (jumping up and down): "Hey, wait! You're gonna die. You need this shot." He tries to push her back down on the bed.

Delise (pushing back): "Stop that. I'm better. I'll be the doctor now."

Nathan (poking her arm with the pretend needle): "You have to get this."

Delise reaches up, punches Nathan, and bursts into tears. Nathan yells, "Teacher! Teacher! Delise hit me! She hit me!" A teacher and three or four children run over from the other side of the room.

The Teacher's Response

The teacher gets down on his knees and puts a firm arm around each child's shoulders, saying, "Delise and Nathan—you're both really upset. What's the problem here?"

Nathan: "Delise hit me!"

Delise: "He gave me a needle—he hurt me."

Nathan: "I had to. I was the doctor!"

Teacher: "Oh. You do have a problem. Doctor Nathan needs to give Patient Delise a needle, but the patient didn't want it—needles can hurt."

Delise (crying): "I hate needles. They give you a lot of needles in the hospital."

Nathan: "I had to, to stop your bleeding heart."

Teacher: "It sounds like you wanted to help Delise get better, Nathan, but needles upset Delise a lot. They feel very unsafe to her. She had to have a lot of needles when she was in the hospital. Even though she had them to help her get better, they hurt and she doesn't want any more." Delise nods. "Can you think of what you could do so you'll feel safe and be happy? We need to figure something out so no one gets hurt."

Delise: "I could be the doctor, not him."

Teacher: "So you could switch jobs? You could be the doctor and Nathan could be the patient?"

Nathan: "I think I should use bandages."

Teacher: "Tell me more. How would that work?"

Nathan: "Use bandages on her heart, no needles. I'll make her better that way. Catch the blood."

Teacher: "Uh huh. You could find another way to make Delise's heart better, without a needle, so she wouldn't be scared of being hurt. What do you think of that idea, Delise? Would that feel safe and okay to do?"

Delise: "Good. I had a lot of bandages when I was in the hospital. And Nathan puts them on good."

Teacher: "Okay, it sounds like Delise wants to try that solution too, Nathan. So let's try it. Make sure you let me know how it works. Now, let's make sure you have the bandages you'll need before I leave. Which one do you need to use first, Nathan?"

At a class meeting later that day, the teacher asks Delise and Nathan to describe their problem and how they worked it out. He hopes to use this as a chance to help all the children think about conflict, but he finds that they all want to talk about their experiences with needles instead. This gives Delise a chance to talk more about her feelings about needles and the other experiences she had in the hospital.

Analysis

Many teachers today report seeing children who seem to be "play deprived"—children who need help learning how to become deeply involved in the play process. These teachers say that the kind of "free play" that has always been central to early childhood settings is becoming harder to promote and maintain; children quickly become bored or their play quickly disintegrates into a dispute. Teachers also report that they're seeing more children who use violence and aggression at the first sign of conflict in play situations than in the past.

There are many factors that help explain these teachers' observations. Increased violence in society and children's increased exposure to it (both directly in their own lives and indirectly through the media) has made violence more central in the ideas that many children build about how people treat each other and deal with problems. In addition, as children spend more time on activities other than play, such as watching television, they have less time to develop the skills that would help them become good players. Less play time can also mean less opportunity to interact with others and develop positive social skills. And when children do have time to play, the highly realistic toys that they often use can promote imitative rather than creative play and lead to a growing dependence on being shown how to play.

To deal with these kinds of problems, adults now need to be more skillful in facilitating the play process than in the past. Many children need help finding interesting activities for play and learning the skills needed for getting and staying involved in a creative play process.

Teachers also play an important role in helping children build the social skills they need in order to engage in meaningful play with others. Without these skills, other efforts to promote constructive and creative play are likely to be less effective; children need to feel safe with each other to be able to fully direct their energies into their play (see Levin, 1995). In the scenarios presented above, the teachers help the children work out their play conflicts and also show the children ways to keep themselves safe and meet their needs without violence.

Social problem-solving skills don't develop in isolation. Children learn social skills from their daily experiences, through a slow process of construction based on their current cognitive levels and abilities. Adults will be most effective when they can link the skills they're trying to teach to the child's direct experiences and base their efforts on an understanding of the developmental concepts and skills of successful conflict resolution (Carlsson-Paige & Levin, 1998).

Conflict resolution skills

Several basic skills are involved in learning to solve conflicts in a nonviolent way; when we try to help children learn these skills, we must take the child's developmental level into account. These skills, and their related developmental issues, include the following:

- ▸ Identifying that there are two (or more) sides to the problem. This requires the child to move from an egocentric to a more decentered perspective.

27

- Recognizing how the actions of each player in the conflict are affecting the behavior of the other players. This challenges a child's ability to make logical, causal connections about their behavior. It requires seeing how each person's actions have contributed to escalating or de-escalating the conflict.

- Coming up with solutions to the problem that satisfy the interests of both or all sides. This challenges children (who focus on the concrete and what they can see) to develop the more abstract skill of imagining what will happen before they concretely try it out.

- Figuring out how to put the agreed-upon solution into practice. This requires that the children work out how all the parts fit together to make a whole, dynamic play activity. The parts include the players, what each player does, the play materials, and the sequence of what happens. It involves converting the "slide" of the solution into a "movie."

- Learning the actual words to use when communicating and working out problems with others. Because of the amount of violence children today are commonly exposed to, many learn to use fighting or fighting words as the first response to a conflict. They need help learning words that they can use to work out their conflicts and that will help them feel powerful without violence.

In each of the first two vignettes, the teachers help the children work on basic conflict-resolution skills in ways that take the children's developmental level and their characteristic thinking into account. As you discuss the teachers' responses, try to identify how the teachers are doing this and how you can apply these ideas to your own work with children. We can use the third vignette to illustrate the following range of issues involved in the teacher's responses:

Text		Commentary
The teacher gets down on his knees and puts a firm arm around each child's shoulders . . .	▶	The teacher uses his body to try to calm the children and reassure them of their safety.
"Delise and Nathan—you're both really upset . . ."	▶	He acknowledges their feelings without passing judgment.
"What's the problem here?"	▶	He brings their focus to defining the problem.
Nathan: "Delise hit me!" Delise: "He gave me a needle—he hurt me." Nathan: "I had to. I was the doctor!"	▶	Nathan and Delise focus on the concrete aspects of the problem (the actual physical actions) from their own egocentric point of view, not as a shared problem.
Teacher: "Oh. You do have a problem. Doctor Nathan needs to give Patient Delise a needle, but the patient didn't want it—needles can hurt."	▶	The teacher helps the children define the problem as a shared one, in concrete terms, from their two points of view.
Delise (crying): "I hate needles. They give you a lot of needles in the hospital."	▶	Delise shows how she is bringing her prior experience into her play; this can help others understand her point of view.
Nathan: "I had to, to stop your bleeding heart."	▶	Nathan tries to explain his point of view. (Nathan does not show possible confusion between the real and unreal.)
Teacher: "It sounds like you wanted to help Delise get better, Nathan, but needles upset Delise a lot. They feel very unsafe to her. She had to have a lot of needles when she was in the hospital. Even though she had them to help her get better, they hurt and she doesn't want any more." Delise nods.	▶	The teacher acknowledges both children's legitimate desires and helps make logical, causal connections between them. In this way, the teacher acts as a transformer—someone who helps the children move from static thinking to cause and effect.
"Can you think of what you could do so you'll feel safe and be happy? We need to figure something out so no one gets hurt."	▶	The teacher focuses the children on coming up with a positive solution that will feel good to both of them.
Delise: "I could be the doctor, not him."	▶	Typical egocentric preschooler focuses on one thing at a time (i.e., what she wants).
Teacher: "So you could switch jobs? You could be the doctor and Nathan could be the patient?"	▶	The teacher serves as transformer for the children, helping them see how Delise's solution would affect both their actions.
Nathan: "I think I should use bandages."	▶	Nathan focuses on what he (not Delise) can do; his response doesn't take Delise's needs into account.
Teacher: "Tell me more. How would that work?"	▶	The teacher tries to get him to elaborate on his ideas and think about how they would translate into practice.
Nathan: "Use bandages on her heart, no needles. I'll make her better that way. Catch the blood."	▶	Nathan shows that he has taken a lot of relevant information into account for his plan.

Using the case materials for group study

Here are some approaches to discussing "Choosing Superhero Roles," "Learning to Take Turns," and "Medical Play Hits a Hurdle."

- ▶ Form small groups to discuss one of the above conflict situations (without the teacher's response) using the discussion questions provided below.
- ▶ Ask each group to share their answers with the whole group and compare the various responses among the groups.
- ▶ Return to small groups to discuss the teacher's response to the conflict, using the second set of discussion questions.
- ▶ Share and discuss the responses of the small groups to the discussion questions. Compare the teacher's responses with the students' original ideas.
- ▶ Review the issues about teaching conflict resolution, and discuss how they are raised by the vignette being discussed (see below).

Possible follow-up activities include the following:

- ▶ Assign students one of the readings about conflict resolution listed under "Additional Readings and Resources."
- ▶ Ask students to apply the concepts of conflict resolution to situations that they are dealing with (or have dealt with) in their work with children, or to one of the other vignettes provided above.
- ▶ Discuss nonplay conflict and problem situations that might come up with children in which the approach used in these vignettes might be effective.

Specific issues raised by each vignette

While the discussion questions can be used with all three vignettes to raise general issues about facilitating play and conflict resolution, each scenario raises unique issues about conflict resolution in play that can help students deepen their understanding and skill at facilitating play.

Choosing Superhero Roles

This vignette can lead to a discussion of how to deal with war and violent play, especially play that is based on media images. Unlike many teachers, the teacher in this vignette has not banned war play altogether. This may surprise some readers. Instead, the teacher helps the children find a way to engage in Power Ranger play that they control and that could help their play expand beyond the narrow scripts that they often imitate on the screen. The teacher feels that adults have a role to play in helping children learn to work through what they see on the screen in a safe way. This vignette can also be used to raise issues about gender differences in children's involvement in war play. (For more on how to deal with war play in a way that promotes healthy play and learning, see Levin and Carlsson-Paige, 1995.)

Learning to Take Turns

This vignette can help readers look at conflict issues related to very young children. For example, the developmental issues involved in helping them learn to "take turns" and function positively in a group can be used to discuss how to approach behavior management in a way that takes the children's developmental levels into account. It also illustrates the very active role that teachers often need to take in helping children learn to try out words, actions, and possible solutions to their problems.

Medical Play Hits a Hurdle

This vignette can help students think about how children's culture and prior experiences (such as Delise's hospitalization) can affect how and what they play, the conflicts that arise in their play, and their ideas about how to work out those conflicts. Students can also discuss how to help children use play to work through stressful or confusing experiences. Another relevant issue is how to encourage girls and boys to play together (Levin, 1994; 1996).

Guidelines for discussing the vignettes

The following discussion guidelines will enable you to practice the same behavior that adults need to use in their problem-solving discussions with children.

- ▶ Create an atmosphere in which it feels safe to express diverse ideas.
- ▶ Encourage differing points of view, rather than trying to find only one right answer.
- ▶ Ask open-ended questions that invite ideas.

- Use a structure (such as the one suggested above) to work on the vignettes, but be prepared and willing to go in unexpected directions based on the issues and needs that come up as the discussion proceeds.

- Plan enough time to hear a wide range of ideas, and for participants to try out their ideas with each other and see where they lead.

- End by identifying ways to apply the ideas to real-life experiences with children.

Discussion Questions

About the conflict

- What is your reaction to this vignette?

- What do you learn about the children in this vignette—their needs, skills, interests, and so forth?

- What ideas do you have about why this situation occurred in the way it did?

- How did the children's levels of development contribute to this conflict?

- How should the teacher have responded during and/or after this situation?

About the teacher's response

- What do you think of the way the teacher dealt with this problem? Was anything about it surprising?

- What do you think about the teacher's solution to this problem? Why?

- How does the teacher's solution compare with how you would have handled this problem?

- Why do you think the teacher approached the problem and the solution in this way?

- As a result of the teacher's response, what information did you learn from the children that helps you better understand them and the problem?

- What do you think the children learned from the teacher's response, and how might that learning affect their play?

Suggested readings and resources
Books
Carlsson-Paige, N. (1998). *Best day of the week*. St. Paul: Redleaf Press.
Carlsson-Paige, N., & Levin, D. (1992). Making peace in violent times: A constructivist approach to conflict resolution. *Young Children, 48* (1), 4–13.
Carlsson-Paige, N., & Levin, D. (1998). *Before push comes to shove: Building conflict resolution skills with young children*. St. Paul: Redleaf Press.
Dinwiddie, S. (1994). The saga of Sally, Sammy, and the red pen: Facilitating children's social problem solving. *Young Children, 49* (5), 13–19.
Jones, E., & Reynolds, G. (1992). *The play's the thing: Teachers' roles in children's play*. New York: Teachers College Press.
Levin, D. E. (1995). Media, culture, & the undermining of play in the United States. In E. Klugman (Ed.) *Play policy and practice*. St. Paul: Redleaf Press.
Wittmer, D., & Honig, A. (1994). Encouraging positive social development in young children. *Young Children, 49* (5), 4–12

Videos
Finch, C., & Wirtanen, L. (2000). *Children and conflict: An opportunity for learning in the early childhood classroom* [Videotape]. Boise, ID: Child Care Connections. Available from Child Care Connections, 1607 West Jefferson Street, Boise, ID 83702.
High/Scope Educational Research Foundation. (1998). *Supporting children in resolving conflicts* [Videotape]. Ypsilanti, MI: Author. Available from High/Scope Educational Research Foundation, 600 North River Street, Ypsilanti, MI 48198.
Latham, R., Sharp, C., & King, K. (1997). *Reframing discipline* [Videotape]. Beaverton, OR: Educational Productions. Available from Educational Productions, 9000 SW Gemini Drive, Beaverton, OR 97008.

Chapter 4

"We Don't Play Like That Here!"
Understanding Aggressive Expressions of Play

Jillian Ardley, Wheelock College (former), and
Lisa Ericson, Wheelock College (former)

Introduction

Through the process of writing a case, student teachers are able to reflect on their teaching practice and construct their knowledge about children's play through meaningful experience. In chapter 5 of *Playing for Keeps: Supporting Children's Play*, Klein (1996) notes that some of the benefits of case writing include professional growth, critical thinking about one's own teaching, engagement in self-governed learning, the ability to frame a problem in its context, and the consideration of multiple perspectives in one case. The only real drawback of using case studies is that students will tend to look for "solutions" for their cases, but solutions are never available (Oldsen & Rudney, 1995). The process of writing a case isn't about finding the "right" answer, because there really aren't any right answers. Instead, it is a process of critically thinking through one's own practice and how to improve it to meet the needs of all the learners in the classroom.

The case below follows one student teacher, "Laura," as she records a case and reflects on it. It shows her development from her original reaction to her thoughts after discussion with other professionals and review of the relevant literature. As you read, put yourself in Laura's shoes as she struggles with her feelings about aggressive play. Share the experience with her as she moves from self-blame to a deeper understanding of children's play and its implications for the teacher.

Certain kinds of perfectly natural play in the classroom strike many beginning teachers as destructive and harmful. Aggressive play, in particular, is worrisome to many adults. However, student teachers are not alone in their concerns about the effects and appropriateness of violent and aggressive play. In a time when eleven- and thirteen-year-old children open fire on their peers in a middle school, it's hard not to worry when we see a child engaging in violent play. Many people believe that violent acts are directly related to how children play with and perceive weapons. For example, in an editorial in the *Washington Post* after a middle-school shooting incident, Judy Mann asked:

> What television shows and movies had they [two middle-school boys who opened fire on their classmates] been watching? What video games did they play? What entertainment did they talk about? What did they read, if anything? (p. T20)

Many teachers express similar responses. "That's why I don't let children play with guns. Children need to respect them as deadly tools," one teacher said. "Kids need to learn early in life that death is real, and weapons and violence bring death." "Too many people ignore that and let kids glorify guns and weapons their whole childhood," another teacher added. When powerful and disturbing events occur, there is always some discussion about who's to blame, and how we might prevent them in the future.

The case that follows shows how Laura thinks through the aggressive play of Aaron, one of the children in her classroom; how her thoughts about aggressive play develop; and how her reactions to Aaron change as she observes, reflects, and seeks help.

Laura's challenge with Aaron

Laura is a student teacher in a kindergarten classroom. As a student teacher, she continually reflects on her practice and evaluates her skills as a teacher. This process includes observing the children in her class as they play. Through these observations, she is learning about her students and how she can best meet their needs as a teacher. At the moment, there's one child in particular whom Laura is worried about: Aaron. He continually plays in a very aggressive and violent way, and often physically hurts other children during play.

Laura teaches in a Quaker school, where passivity and nonviolence are two of the key tenets. So she must grapple with the issue of how to deal with Aaron's aggressive play in a setting where violence is not accepted. She's left wondering: "How can I help Aaron express his aggressive feelings in a way that is safe, acceptable, and effective? How can I balance the Quaker beliefs with what appear to be the naturally aggressive tendencies of certain children?"

Student teachers such as Laura question the effects of violent play even when there are no social events to bring the topic to the surface. They may worry that aggressive play in their classroom is a reflection of a lack of management or preparation skills on their part. This is one of the reasons why the words "We don't play like that here!" can often be heard in Laura's room. Raised voices and roughhousing—play characterized by falling upon one another—is frowned upon both by the school's founders and by the teacher in the next room.

Looking at aggressive and violent play means looking at the content and actions of a child's active play. However, it isn't only the child's physical movements that make an activity aggressive or violent: fluid constructive play in which aggressive behaviors are dramatized, such as in a drawing, can also be deemed a form of aggressive or violent play. Aaron concerns Laura in this way, too, because he depicts his aggressive and violent thoughts in pictures as well as dramatizing them through physical acts.

Aaron turned six in January. He loves to draw, read, move, and interact with his friends. Aaron's play tends to be rough, and can be violent. This is becoming a concern in the classroom, because an increasing number of children have been physically hurt by him, which makes him seem like a bully.

Although Aaron is from a Quaker family, he still engages in play that is centered on violence. He's aware that Quakers don't use weapons, as shown by a remark he made near the beginning of the year: "I'm a Quaker, except that I have weapons." He likes to practice karate kicks and chops, and he enjoys pretending to use weapons, especially swords. Aaron is very physical. His play often seems aggressive, because he loves to wrestle and tumble on the ground with his friends in the playground. He never intends to hurt anyone; he just enjoys playing this way. He hugs his friends a lot, but the hugs can be very rough.

On the other hand, Aaron can also be very thoughtful. He spends a great deal of time doing projects, especially drawings. He uses a lot of details in his work, and has a hard time stopping if he isn't finished. His drawings are complex and often show muscular people (mostly men) in armor. Most of his pictures have some sort of weapon in them, usually a sword. When he draws these pictures he begins with the weapons, and then draws outward from there.

Aaron struggles with play entry. He doesn't usually initiate play with others in a positive way. He often grabs things from other children; he will watch a game and get really angry if he sees that the other children aren't following the rules that are familiar to him. He has a hard time being patient in these situations, and will yell, cry, and sometimes hit the person who isn't "playing right."

Aaron is interested in playing with others and committed to his friendships. He shows an intense affection for one child in particular, named Stephen. The two boys have a great interest in drawing and playing games that center on Greek gods and medieval times. Both children come from Quaker families, and attend the same Meeting on Sundays. Aaron plays with Stephen most often, and it is during their play that many of his aggressive acts occur. Stephen has a hard time defining limits with Aaron, and their aggressive play often leads to Stephen being physically injured.

The following vignettes describe the violence that Laura has observed in Aaron's play and how she responded to them:

Playing Superheroes

Laura notices that Aaron and Stephen are playing a game in which they are both superheroes: Stephen is "Laserman" and Aaron is "Wolfdog." (Laserman and Wolfdog are superheroes that they have invented themselves on the playground.) The two boys are running around the playground fighting invisible supervillains. Stephen, as Laserman, is shooting lasers from his hands at the "bad guys," and Aaron, as Wolfdog, is jumping toward them with his sharp claws and fierce teeth, while running and making huge strides.

Laura believes that this type of superhero play isn't really okay, so she pauses to evaluate whether she should step in and stop the game. However, before she can decide, something happens that makes it necessary for her to step in—Laserman and Wolfdog suddenly become enemies instead of allies. Aaron tells Stephen that it isn't fun to chase an invisible villain and declares that he will be the villain and that Stephen has to catch him. Stephen is now shooting his lasers at Aaron. Now Laura has to intercede, because she believes that it is definitely not acceptable for children to shoot at other children. However, as she begins to call out "Stephen and Aaron!" and make her way toward them, Aaron (Wolfdog) leaps onto Stephen (Laserman) and grabs his neck, snarling loudly as they both fall to the ground—Aaron on top of Stephen, with his hands still around his neck.

Laura starts yelling, "Stop right now! Aaron, get off of him now! Right now!" She has to pull Aaron off of Stephen. Stephen is crying and Aaron is laughing. She says quickly, "Aaron, go and take a break on the bench. It's never okay to put your hands on another person's neck. I will not allow that." She then turns to hug Stephen, who is still crying. Aaron stomps his feet and scowls at her. He declares, "It was the game. Wolfdog pounces on the bad guy. Besides, he was shooting me. How come he isn't in trouble? Remember, no guns at school!"

"Yes," Laura replies, "I was just coming over here to tell him that, but he didn't really hurt you. You were on him and hurting his neck. That is not okay. I don't want to see either of you playing that superhero game again. That game is too rough. We don't have superheroes at school." Aaron kicks the ground, grits his teeth, and answers with a deep scowl, "Fine!" He stomps over to the bench and sits down.

Although the problem is sort of resolved, Stephen is left crying, Aaron is mad, and Laura feels like a mean teacher. She doesn't feel at all like the problem is really resolved. She knows deep down that it will happen again, but she still hopes that it won't.

The Restaurant

Aaron, Stephen, and Michael are playing in the "house corner," pretending that it is a restaurant. They have invited Laura to the restaurant for a nice lunch, and she has gladly accepted the invitation. She makes herself comfortable at the table, and begins to order a meal. She turns and looks at Aaron, who is playing the chef. He begins to tell her the menu and she tells him what she would like. While he cooks her meal, Stephen and

Michael give her some dolls and tell her that she's their mother. As she gently holds the dolls and awaits her meal, she notices that Aaron is roughly pulling the clothes off another doll. When the doll is fully unclothed, he opens the pretend oven door and throws the baby inside. He shuts the door and turns the "heat" knob all the way up. Laura looks at him and asks, baffled, "Why did you do that, Aaron?"

"Well, I'm cooking the baby up," he answers.

"Why?"

"I don't know. I just wanted to," he responds. Laura decides to view this action in the context of play. She has heard one of her professors say that a situation where a child is pretending to hurt someone may be an opportunity to build empathy for the person who's being hurt. So she decides to respond from that perspective.

"The baby will be burned up. I'd better call an ambulance fast. I don't want the baby to die," she says, pretending to call an ambulance. "Yeah, we have an emergency here. There's a baby in the oven. Can you send an ambulance to help the baby?"

Aaron looks up and smiles. He says, "The ambulance blew up. There was a bomb in it."

Laura looks at him and says, "Oh no, that's very sad. Maybe I should call another ambulance."

"That won't work, because the phone just blew up, too. There was a bomb in the phone. Besides, the baby is dead already. He got all burned up," Aaron says and laughs.

At this point Laura has no idea what to do. She trudges on, saying, "That's really sad. I wish we could have helped the baby. I think that from now on cooking babies will not be an okay game for anyone to play at school. It's a scary game."

Aaron looks at Laura with disgust, and then turns his head away from her, snorting "Hmmph!"

As Laura leaves the house corner, she feels baffled, confused, and upset. Is it really okay to have a game where a baby is cooked and an ambulance is bombed? This play behavior does not seem good to her. Although no one was actually hurt, the scene made her feel uneasy. She leaves with a sick feeling in the pit of her stomach and the realization that she has banned yet another of Aaron's violent games. She wonders whether this was the correct response. "Did I do the right thing? Is this just another developmentally appropriate play [scenario] in which a child is trying to handle his anxiety or feelings about his environment? Bottom line, I don't really understand this type of behavior—and not knowing how to deal with it really bothers me."

Laura's concerns

These vignettes show just a few highlights of aggression in Aaron's play, and the difficulties Laura has had dealing with it. He will also sometimes engage in weapon play, but not very often. He is much more likely to draw weapons, or people using weapons, than to act out the use of weapons. This should probably give Laura a feeling of relief. But she is actually more worried about her relationship with Aaron than with her ability to be seen as a practitioner who knows developmentally appropriate practices.

Laura is also concerned about the safety of the other children in the classroom, and how Aaron's aggressive play will affect his relationships with his peers. She feels that this is a major social and emotional issue for him, and always leaves their interactions wondering how she can help him: "It seems as if he can only play in ways that are rough and aggressive. If he continues like this, he won't have any willing playmates left. I need help in dealing with this situation. What should I have done? What should I do now?"

Reflections at the end of the year

By the end of the kindergarten year, Aaron had begun to reduce his hostile, aggressive play activities. With her cooperating teacher, Laura designed a sticker chart to reward Aaron when he played with his friends in a safe way. This was somewhat helpful. More important, Laura refrained from interfering in his play as often. She started to offer Aaron suggestions to help, rather than restrict, his play. For example, one afternoon while the children were playing outside, she observed Aaron following some children around and making karate chops at them. The children weren't paying any attention to him. Aaron was getting close to them, and Laura could see that he wanted them to notice him. She asked him: "Do you want to play with them?"

He said, "Yes, but they won't let me."

"Did you ask them if you could play?" Laura asked. Aaron shook his head and sighed.

"Well, just go up to them and say 'Can I play?' and see what they say," Laura suggested.

Aaron turned and ran to the other children and did exactly what Laura suggested—and it worked! He asked, and they said "sure" and let him choose who he wanted to be in their game. Laura realized that "Aaron didn't need me to tell him to stop karate chopping. He needed me to guide him in how to join the play. He wasn't sure how, and I offered support that was nonjudgmental."

The end of the year was filled with more positive interactions such as this one. However, there were still moments that were difficult. Laura wrote in her journal that

> Aaron will continue to need positive support, and the chance to express aggression in a healthy way. He is enrolled in karate, which hopefully will help him learn about self control and give him an outlet for some of his aggression. In addition, his parents are looking into play groups that focus on learning how to play with other children in positive ways. The school and the parents are very invested in helping him channel his aggression, and helping him have positive experiences in social play. This commitment is comforting to me, and I feel confident that he will improve his social play skills.

> As for me, my year as a student teacher has ended. I am now certified to teach on my own, and as I reflect back over the year, I am thinking a lot about who I am as a teacher and as a person. Even though teaching is a profession with certain commonalities for all teachers, my experiences within this profession are very personal. I thought a lot this year about where I come from, and what school was like for me. I know that the way I react to children in my classroom is strongly based on my own school experiences. As a child I was very quiet and well behaved. I had few friends, and I hardly ever disobeyed my teacher. (Laura's journal notes, 1998)

Commentary

We cannot divorce a person from their past or present circumstances. We can tell them what we believe to be appropriate, but to understand Laura's challenge, we must respect her feelings and her search for the truth. Throughout the semester Laura struggled with the issues raised by her experiences with Aaron. She talked with colleagues and read some of the literature on violence in children's play. She came to see that

Although Aaron hurts people in his play, he does not intend it. I think his play is more of the natural aggression with a little hostility at times. For the most part, I think that his aggression is more a way he gains control over situations. I am finding that I really think this aggressive aspect of his play is important in his growth and development. However, it is also clear that he needs some help in doing this.

I am now seeing how I need to help him channel his aggressive play into more constructive forms of aggressive play. I see now that banning certain types of play is not helping him. (Laura's journal notes, 1998)

Laura learned that although aggressive behavior is common, it must be dealt with. In this case, the beliefs of the school and of Aaron's Quaker parents, Laura's past experiences with aggressive play, and her present knowledge of appropriate play had to be factored into the solution. It took time, not just book knowledge, for Laura to realize that her interrupting Aaron's play was only changing his attitude toward her.

The fear of violence or aggressive play is really an adult issue. This child is being brought up in the Quaker tradition; he's being raised to value nonviolent behavior. However, he chooses to participate in fantasy play that is aggressive. Perhaps he's trying to demonstrate through such acts that he's the one in control of his behavior or his environment. Maybe he wants to participate in something that is taboo in his religion. His behavior might be due to a variety of reasons, and sometimes children cannot voice their rationale for their behavior. So we must take the focus off ourselves, observe the child, and ask:

- Is the child hurting anyone?
- Does his aggressive behavior keep him from participating in play schemes with friends?
- Is he disrespecting the rules of his environment?

If the answers to these questions are yes, as in Aaron's case, the teacher should become proactive rather than reactive.

Being proactive means thinking about the situation in advance and identifying alternative ways of dealing with the issue before the behavior occurs. It can also mean reflecting on our own feelings or bias toward the behavior and the child in question to see if the chosen techniques are appropriate in this case. When teachers take the time for these important steps, their practices are less likely to clash with the values and practices of the school and the child's parents.

In Aaron's case, Laura was able to use the following approaches to facilitate play that was acceptable to her and that conformed to the school's norms and policies:

- ▶ Initiate imaginative play sequences to model appropriate aggressive behaviors.
- ▶ Consult resources (books and software) about effective and ineffective play behavior. (See the suggested readings at the end of this chapter.)
- ▶ Role-play how it feels to be the victim of violent forms of play, possibly with the guidance of a journal or person who is well versed in play therapy.
- ▶ Meet with colleagues and the child's parents to discuss alternative approaches that will help the student.
- ▶ Look within the child's community for insight to their beliefs about play.

Above all, remember that you are trying to train children to live effectively within the global community. So, if at all possible, let them "play it out." Children can't learn appropriate play and social skills if you don't allow them to become involved in interpersonal conflict that they must learn to resolve on their own (Beaty, 1995). This doesn't mean leaving the situation and letting them fight it out. Instead, it means becoming a respectful observer who intervenes when necessary.

As children practice their socialization skills through imaginative play, they discover what is and is not acceptable to their peers. For example, although Aaron thought that the games "sucked" when the other children didn't play "right," he would grudgingly decide to play their way when he would otherwise be isolated. He will soon get the point that hostile and aggressive play won't be tolerated by his classmates.

Conclusion

It was not Aaron who needed the most work this year; it was Laura. By working through her concerns and misconceptions about aggressive play, Laura learned to appreciate the energy that Aaron brought to the class. She learned to respect the school's philosophy of nonviolence and help Aaron play in a less aggressive fashion. By engaging in the process of writing a case about a child with whom she had difficulty, Laura not only learned about the meaning of play, but also gained insight into her own belief system about aggressive play, a powerful force in any teacher's practice.

Aggressive play should not surprise a society that idolizes the toughest kid on the block and pays top dollar to see a famous actor or actress blow up a city. However, to maintain order in class, teachers cannot tolerate certain forms of aggressiveness. Children do not always know where and when to draw the line, especially when they are admired for the same behavior in their community. It is the teacher's responsibility to teach children how to negotiate social norms so that they can be successful not only in school, but also in the broader society. Understanding the aspects and implications of aggressive play is not an option but a necessity for a teacher who is interested in the success of all children.

Discussion Questions

This case is about a teacher who is trying to balance her personal beliefs and attitudes with the cultural beliefs and norms of her school. In the following discussion questions, you will first consider the perspective of each character, including the cultural perspective of Aaron's parents. Next, you will describe to your group how *you* perceive aggression and violence in school. (Don't skip this step! It will help you and your peers understand the origin of your ideas and opinions.) Finally, you will propose an approach to solving the problem posed in this case.

Aaron

- ▸ What do you know about Aaron's background?
- ▸ How does Aaron's aggressive play affect his relationships with other children?
- ▸ What issue(s) might Aaron's parents address with him?
- ▸ How might Aaron's parents feel about their son's behavior?

Laura

- ▸ What are Laura's attitudes toward the school? Toward the families of the children? Toward teaching?
- ▸ How does Laura define the problem?
- ▸ What strategies does Laura seem to use to change Aaron's behavior?
- ▸ How effective is she at changing his behavior?

You

- What is your attitude toward aggressive play?
- What has been your response toward violence in school?
- What would you have done if you had been in Laura's place?
- How could Laura speak to the school community (including the parents) in a way that is respectful of their beliefs, without sidestepping her own beliefs and views about appropriate play?
- What would you recommend that Laura do further to resolve her ambivalence about Aaron's behavior?
- What types of support networks and resources might be helpful to Laura in this particular sociocultural setting?

Suggested readings and resources

Canada, G. (1995). *Fist stick knife gun: A personal history of violence in America.* Boston: Beacon Press.

Carlsson-Paige, N., & Levin, D. (1987). *The war play dilemma: Balancing needs and values in the early childhood classroom.* New York: Teachers College Press.

Carlsson-Paige, N., & Levin, D. (1990). *Who's calling the shots? How to respond effectively to children's fascination with war play and war toys.* Philadelphia: New Society.

Carlsson-Paige, N., Levin, D., & Henriquez, C. (1998). *Before push comes to shove: Building conflict resolution skills with children.* St. Paul: Redleaf Press.

Cherry, C. (1983). *Please don't sit on the kids.* Belmont, CA: Pitman.

Funk, J., & Buchman, D. (2000). Preference for violent electronic games, self-concept, and gender differences in young children. *American Journal of Orthopsychiatry, 70* (2), 233–241.

Guetzloe, E., & Rockwell, S. (1998). Fight, flight, or better choices: Teaching nonviolent responses to young children. *Preventing School Failure, 42* (4), 154–159.

Jones, E., & Reynolds, G. (1992). *The play's the thing: Teachers' roles in children's play.* New York: Teachers College Press.

Karr-Moss, R., & Wiley, M. (1999). *Ghosts from the nursery: Tracing the roots of violence.* New York: Atlantic Monthly Press.

Katch, J. (2001). *Under deadman's skin: Discovering the meaning of children's violent play.* Boston: Beacon Press.

Kreidler, W. (1984). *Creative conflict resolution: More than 200 activities for keeping peace in the classroom.* Glenview, IL: Scott, Foresman.

Levine, M. (1998). *See no evil: A guide to protecting our children from media violence.* San Francisco: Jossey-Bass.

Morrow, L. (1998). Tragedy as child's play. *Time*, *151* (13), 82.

Nathanson, A. (1999). Identifying and explaining the relationship between parental mediation and children's aggression. *Communication Research, 26* (2), 124–143.

Piers, M., & Landau, G. (1980). *The gift of play and why young children cannot thrive without it*. New York: Walker.

Varney, W. (2000). Playing with 'war fare.' *Peace Review, 12* (3), 385–391.

William, P. (1999). *Real boys: Rescuing our sons from the myths of boyhood*. New York: Owl Books.

Section 2

▶▶▶▶▶▶▶▶▶▶▶▶▶▶▶▶▶▶▶▶▶

Cultural Differences

Chapter 5

What's Wrong with Playing Cowboys and Indians?
Teaching Cultural Diversity to Preschoolers

Amelia Klein, Wheelock College, with commentary by
Carol J. Mills, Wheelock College (former)

Introduction

This chapter presents a narrative case that can be used as a learning tool to enhance cultural sensitivity in professionals who work in the field of early care and education. The case is designed to be used for discussion purposes, using the case method approach to teaching and learning. Case methodology provides an interactive group format that can generate critical thinking, collaborative problem solving, and knowledge construction in adult learners. For an in-depth perspective on the case method and its usefulness in preparing early childhood educators, see chapter 5 of *Playing for Keeps: Supporting Children's Play* (Klein, 1996).

Under the guidance of a discussion leader, the participants in a case discussion are challenged to examine the multiple perspectives of a conflict situation embedded in a case. In the case that follows, these multiple perspectives consist of conflicting opinions about the portrayal of Native Americans in children's sociodramatic play. The setting for the case is a preschool classroom consisting of three-year-olds, their teacher, a student intern, and the intern's college supervisor (a visitor and critical observer). The case consists of a play episode that occurs during one of the supervisor's visits to the classroom.

The case presented here focuses on two controversial beliefs: that children do not take pretend play "seriously" (that is, that what they do does not represent what they think), and that play and the use of play materials does not affect children's conceptual development or learning.

The goal of this case is to examine play as a medium for cultural learning. To further this goal, it is accompanied by a commentary from Native American consultant and educator Carol Mills. The case is followed by an analysis of beliefs about the nature of play and the process through which children develop concepts about diverse cultural groups, such as American Indian people. The discussion that follows the case also provides recommendations for engaging discussants in examining their own use of play as a medium for cultural learning.

Several of the chapters in *Playing for Keeps* provide a framework for this chapter. Chapter 1 explores the range of knowledge, beliefs, and values about play, and the relationship between play and various aspects of cognitive development (McLane & Spielberger, 1996). The authors examine early childhood professionals' knowledge about play, and demonstrate how belief shapes practice. Chapter 2 examines perceptions of play held by college students whose beliefs are shaped by their own memories of play (Klugman, 1996). Chapters 6 and 7 look at factors that negatively affect children's cognitive and social development, such as media-linked toys and media-defined images (Levin, 1996; Cooper, 1996). The authors of chapter 8 advocate "a more systematic and careful examination of the social and cultural contexts of children's play" (Meier & Murrell, 1996).

In the process of examining the meaning of play for young children, child care providers and early childhood teachers must examine the cultural context and early childhood experiences that have shaped their own beliefs and opinions about diversity. It is hoped that the case will provide a starting point for self-reflection.

The Magic Kingdom Early Learning Center

The Magic Kingdom Early Learning Center is located in a suburb of a large northeastern city in the United States. The school provides early care and education for children between three and five years old, serving a population of primarily white, upper-middle-class families. The center also receives student interns from local colleges and universities, who are enrolled in teacher education programs and are required to complete intensive fieldwork as part of their professional training. As interns in the preschool classroom, these college students must demonstrate their knowledge of developmentally and culturally appropriate practice. In addition, they have an opportunity to test their understanding of the concepts and standards that are fundamental to the philosophy of early childhood education. The Magic Kingdom Early Learning Center is a setting in which these student interns can increase their knowledge about teaching through practice and reflection.

Most members of the center, including the teachers, parents, interns, and children, have never been to a Native American cultural event or met a Native American person. Informal interviews with residents of the community have indicated that the interviewees believe that Indian people no longer inhabit their region, with the exception of a few isolated communities in rural areas. They believe that in order to have contact with "real" American Indians, they would have to travel to other parts of the country, such as the southwestern United States. In addition, very few of those interviewed were able to name any of the Indian nations indigenous to their region.

Playing "Cowboys and Indians"

It is Monday morning. Douglas, a student teacher who is assigned to a classroom of three-year-olds, is busy setting up materials before the children arrive. Today he will begin a unit on "Indians." Douglas has placed an assortment of thematic materials in various places throughout the classroom. The sandbox contains small two-dimensional figures of "cowboys" and "Indians." The Indian figures are all holding weapons—a bow and arrow or a tomahawk—and appear to be engaged in fighting. In other areas of the room Douglas has placed storybooks, puzzles, pictures, dress-up clothes (such as a headdress of "eagle" feathers, moccasins, beads, and deerskins) and a large tepee with a "campfire" in the middle. All these materials depict Native Americans (without referring to any specific nations) in stereotypical ways. The materials suggest that contemporary American Indian people live a primitive existence, that they are all savages or warriors, and that all Native Americans are alike.

Once the children arrive, Douglas brings them together for a large group meeting and introduces the topic of "Indians." He teaches the children the song "Ten Little Indians." He then directs the children to various areas of the room and encourages them to interact with the materials he has provided. Many of the children engage in war play, making war cries and pretending that they are "fighting the Indians."

All these activities are observed by Douglas' college supervisor, who is present in the classroom to observe Douglas' efforts in planning and implementing multicultural learning experiences for young children.

The college supervisor's observations

The supervisor was astounded and confused—why was Douglas teaching about Native Americans in this way? The topic of teaching diversity had been covered in a seminar that Douglas took several weeks before this curriculum unit began. During this intensive seminar, which was taught by the supervisor, the students explored methods of teaching children about cultural diversity in an accurate, sensitive, and nonstereotypical way. In his written assignment for the seminar, Douglas had effectively articulated the points of view of nationally known authors on the philosophy and framework of anti-bias curriculum. As a student intern, Douglas was expected to apply these principles to his own curriculum planning.

The topic of cultural diversity had also been addressed in other courses that Douglas had completed before he began student teaching, including a course on multicultural education. The instructor had invited guest speakers from various cultural groups (including prominent American Indian people) to class seminars to provide students with a cultural lens different from their own. The students had opportunities to interact with the guest speakers and clarify the issues associated with teaching children about diversity. They had also learned about Native peoples in contemporary society. Douglas, like the other students in his multicultural class, had assumed that the world he lived in was different from that of Native American people. After viewing a film about Native American children on a reservation, he had expressed surprise that the children lived in "houses like mine," went to school on a school bus, attended traditional kindergarten or nursery school classes, and dressed "just like my younger brothers or sisters."

The supervisor wondered why Douglas' teaching and learning strategies did not reflect the concepts and values that had been emphasized in this core course, as well as throughout the entire teacher education program.

Douglas' point of view

Douglas considered his methods to be appropriate. His rationale was that he was exposing the children to American history and folklore in a concrete way (that is, a developmentally appropriate practice). He stated that the materials and activities that he had introduced to the children would only be considered offensive by some Native American people. He believed that objections to this "traditional" depiction of Native Americans reflected a radical or extreme—as well as unpatriotic—point of view.

Douglas felt comfortable sharing the same kind of information that had been shared with American schoolchildren for generations. He recalled with pleasure how he had learned about "the Indians" in elementary school and had played with objects similar to those he had brought into this classroom. As a young boy, he and his friends had engaged in imaginative play about Indians and had constructed tepees in his backyard. He had been fascinated by books about brave Indian warriors and wise Indian chiefs. He had yearned to live in the wilderness, close to nature, and to be strong and self-sufficient. Indians had been his superheroes and models as he was growing up. What could be wrong with teaching this perspective?

Douglas said that he had been encouraged and supported by the other teachers and the parents at the center to present this perspective on American Indian life. He cited textbooks, children's books, and teacher's manuals ("written by experts") that supported his approach. After all, he wasn't biased against Indians—his respect for their culture was earnest, and he wanted to pass that respect on to his young pupils.

Although Douglas was aware that some Native American people or educators might disagree with him, he felt that there was no harm in children engaging in the play situations that he was promoting in the classroom. After all, the children were "just playing" and imitating what they had seen on television or in picture books. Why should this innocent and imaginative play behavior result in negative impressions about Indians?

Commentary by Carol Mills

To begin with, there are many tribes living in the northeastern part of the United States, contrary to the beliefs of this community. Before the arrival of the Europeans, the region in which the center is located was the sacred land of Native American people, and Indian people continue to live on their original land as they did in the 1600s. Today Native American people, their culture, and their traditions are an integral part of many of the communities in the area. They regularly hold powwows, many of which are open to the public. Visitors to these powwows can view traditional dancing and drumming and purchase items at craft and resource tables.

Many museums in the area provide accurate information about the historical and contemporary cultural life of the local indigenous peoples. National and regional Indian organizations in the area provide information to those who wish to learn about current affairs. The tribal councils in the region provide guidance and support for Indian people and can serve as resources for the general public. The local colleges and universities have many Native American students and active Native American associations and programs, as well as Indian centers and organizations that provide cultural and social service support for Indian students while they are away from home. Many of these students regularly return to their home reservation to maintain their strong ties with their family and culture.

For many years, mainstream society has been defining and redefining who Indians are. Even the politically correct term *Native American* implies that we all desire to be called the same thing and is another way that society has sought to identify us as a generic group of people. However, there are many cultural differences between our nations. Our widely different geographical environments dictate our differing lifestyles, languages, and customs.

Over the years, Hollywood images have very effectively distorted the truths about Native peoples; the negative stereotypical images shown on film are ingrained in our memories. One-sided textbooks have also contributed to our cultural genocide. We have had to struggle to maintain our visibility within the American school system. Many Native communities have had the challenge of forcing change within the local school system, typically regarding issues such as historical inaccuracies and the neglect of Native American history. European values and history are integrated throughout the curriculum, and the values and culture of the original inhabitants of this continent should be represented as well. All American schoolchildren are entitled to hear the truth and to be taught accurate historical facts.

Many Native American parents are concerned about the negative portrayal of Indian people in children's books. Besides the one-sided perspective, Native culture and peoples are referred to as a past entity, as opposed to a vibrant, living, contributing group of people.

Our communities have a responsibility to reach out to institutions that have successfully made positive changes within the educational system on our behalf. These collaborations and partnerships are examples of how racism can be slowly eliminated from our schools and eventually our lives. Some Indian people are resistant to sharing their culture with others. In the past, the facts have been distorted and information has been misinterpreted. In some cases, monetary gain was the ulterior motive. However, there are some genuinely concerned educators who are helping to dispel the myths and stereotypes about us. They have taken the time to learn and respect our values and perspectives, and the impact they have on child development.

Anti-bias approaches to this case

The discussion questions in the next section describe how a discussion leader can help a group examine the specific issues raised in the case. This section presents the major variables that should be considered in analyzing the case, which can provide a framework for the case discussion. It will focus on anti-bias curriculum—its theoretical orientation and practical applications—as a framework for interpreting Douglas' actions. Participants would benefit from having this background information before discussing the case. The references cited could be used as reading assignments to prepare for the case discussion. (Another approach would be to assign the readings after the discussion, so that participants could use them to verify or extend their thinking about the issues raised in the case discussion by "learning through discovery.")

Sources of children's concepts about diversity
Family members and teachers

Children bond closely with significant people in their lives. Young children's perspectives on diversity are largely influenced by the beliefs and behaviors of family members and teachers (Ramsey, 1987; Seefeldt, 1997).

These significant people have the power to help children learn about cultural differences, either positively or negatively.

The prevailing attitudes of parents and siblings provide a model for children to follow and also influence their perceptions of people who are different from themselves. Young children develop negative concepts of Indian people when family members reinforce stereotypical images. For example, families who purchase "Indian" Halloween costumes for their children, or provide them with toys and books that promote stereotypes, are helping their children construct culturally insensitive and inaccurate knowledge about Indian people.

Teachers can nurture the development of stereotypes by misrepresenting Native peoples through songs ("Ten Little Indians"), actions ("Sit Indian-style"), pictures (alphabet charts that associate the letter "I" with a picture of an "Indian," or the letter "E" with a picture of an "Eskimo"), and classroom events (having children dress up as pilgrims and Indians for a Thanksgiving feast).

The media

Children are exposed to various media, such as television, films, videos, and computer software. These means of communication have a strong influence on young children, who are not capable of differentiating fantasy from reality. For example, children construct negative images of culturally diverse people as a result of watching cartoons embedded with stereotypical images (Cortés, 2000; Hesse & Poklemba, 1994).

Children's books and magazines

Children's books and magazines can also be sources of inaccurate or misleading information about Indian people and their history (Slapin & Seale, 1992). When their books only portray American Indians in the past, children have difficulty understanding that Native people still exist. Because many of the images that children see of Indian people are illustrations or drawings, children are unable to attribute human qualities to them, or to see them as individuals with universal traits. Early childhood educators and researchers have cautioned teachers about exposing very young children to stereotypical portrayals before the children have developed an understanding of "self" and "others" (Dowd, 1992).

The social environment

Children are influenced by the symbols, objects, and behavior that they observe in their social environment. Young children may be exposed to stereotypes and caricatures of Native Americans in advertisements, greeting cards, calendars, sports logos, exhibits, food packages, and other stimuli in the world around them. A teddy bear wearing a feather headdress and a cartoon figure dressed as an "Indian princess" on a birthday card will both reinforce stereotypical images. When children observe sports fans doing a "tomahawk chop" or "Indian dance" on an athletic field, they receive the message that adults find these actions to be acceptable and entertaining.

Ways to change children's concepts about diversity

Use play as a medium for cultural learning

As children play, they express their knowledge of the world. Play materials are important resources for children's learning (Moyles, 1990). Children manipulate play materials not only to test their ideas, but also to experiment with new ones. Play objects are children's links to "reality." Through careful observation of play behavior, teachers can determine children's knowledge and attitudes about a particular cultural or racial group, and also provide experiences that challenge any biased views.

Reading books about contemporary Indian life during story time is one way to provide accurate information that children can then integrate into their play themes in a positive way (see additional readings and resources at the end of this chapter). Providing books and photographs that depict present-day Indian people will make children aware that Native peoples dress and act like them, although they may have different customs or traditions. Pictures and props that represent the contemporary Indian life of specific cultures (such as dolls, music tapes, wild rice sticks and baskets, rocks for a clambake, maple syrup containers and molds, and so on) can be added to the "housekeeping" sociodramatic play area. The children will explore these materials as they reconstruct everyday life experiences, such as getting food for dinner, taking care of babies, or listening to music.

Implement an anti-bias curriculum

Active intervention by a teacher (such as integrating cultural diversity in an honest, natural, and personally meaningful way in the context of play) can change children's negative concepts about another group. A more global perspective involves influencing the environment in which children play by creating an anti-bias culture in their classrooms that prepares children "to grow up with the attitudes, knowledge, and skills necessary for effective living in a complex, diverse world" and that actively challenges "the impact of bias on children's development" (Derman-Sparks, 1989, p. 5). In her classic text, Derman-Sparks highlights ways that teachers can develop an anti-bias curriculum by focusing on the visual/aesthetic aspects of the classroom environment, toys and materials, and ways of modeling fairness, empathy, and respect. Others have identified developmentally appropriate anti-bias skills and tools to help young children recognize and criticize stereotyping (Hall, 1999; Lee et al., 1998).

Examine your own beliefs and knowledge about diversity

"Preschool teachers don't teach the essence of what is Native American because we don't know the Native American culture. . . . We need Native Americans to tell us if material is authentic, is nonstereotypical, and captures the essence of the culture" (Billman, 1992, p. 22). These words of a non–Native American teacher reflect the challenge that early childhood educators face when they attempt to teach children about diverse groups in a culturally sensitive way. In order to have an effective multicultural and anti-bias curriculum, teachers must engage in research: first, they must examine their own knowledge and teaching behavior; and second, they must examine the values, beliefs, and perspectives of the cultural groups they are teaching about (Cornelius, 1998; De Gaetano et al., 1998; Hernandez, 2001).

Bridge the gap between theory and practice

Advocates of multicultural education must address the question, "Why is it important for teachers to know themselves, to examine their own attitudes and values toward other people?" (Seefeldt, 1997, chapter 10). One answer is that challenging and exploring our habitual attitudes and beliefs creates a state of cognitive dissonance that can lead to growth and development of thought. A person can either justify the preexisting point of view or explore the basis for that belief and gain new knowledge. When done in a group setting, this self-reflective process is most effective in a safe and supportive environment (Ramsey, 1987). Anti-bias teacher training programs that take this factor into consideration are effective in promoting cultural sensitivity and self-awareness (Carter & Curtis, 1994; Hyun, 1998).

One activity that can help teachers bridge the gap between theory and practice is to construct "lesson plans" for the play activities they introduce into their classroom. Through the process of articulating (a) developmentally and culturally appropriate goals and objectives; (b) the nature of play experiences; (c) the children's learning behavior; and (d) new goals based on their findings, teachers will need to logically relate all relevant issues into their curriculum planning.

Inform yourself about diversity

There are many ways for teachers to learn about American Indian people and other cultural groups. The opportunities for learning include

- talking directly to Indian people
- locating Indian cultural resources in the telephone book
- visiting local Native American centers
- establishing links to Indian education projects in the local public schools (GossMan, 1992) or universities
- browsing the Internet (Web sites such as *http://www.nativeweb.org* and *http://www.oyate.org*. OYATE is a national organization that provides accurate information about Native peoples and is a resource for Native American publications) and visiting museums that offer resources organized by the indigenous people of the region

Use the K-W-L approach

Applying the principles of early childhood education to your own practice can help you think objectively about your own cultural knowledge and reflect on your practice. By using the approach that early childhood educators commonly refer to as K-W-L, teachers can assess what they themselves *know* (K), what they are *wondering* about (W), and what they need to *learn* (L). This process can help teachers create a perspective from which to view the events in their classrooms. Greenberg (1992) has suggested the following three goals for teachers who wish to pursue multicultural and anti-bias education:

- ▶ Stop being culturally assaultive.
- ▶ Stop benignly tolerating erroneous, erasing, insulting, and discriminatory behavior on the part of others.
- ▶ Start making classrooms inclusive, as befits schools in a democracy.

Develop practices that are appropriate for all children

The learning community in the case presented above did not include any Native children. How might teachers of young children broaden their perspective of developmentally appropriate, culturally sensitive practice to include Native American children and their families? What must early childhood educators know in order to construct an inclusive curriculum that integrates Native American values and learning styles?

Conclusion by Carol Mills

When I talk to students who are entering the field of teaching, I recommend that they reassess their own values before they start teaching young children. For example, since Native American children often prefer to learn by first observing rather than doing, the hands-on approach may not be the best method for all children. Traditional Indian teachings include observation and watching behavior that is modeled by our parents, grandparents, aunts, and uncles, as well as other tribal members. Once a child has demonstrated interest and respect, he or she may be invited to sit at the drum and sing, be given some clay to mold, be asked to help make fry bread for the feast, or join the older men to go hunting.

Indian children learn about social roles during their play, which is their work for later life. Some Native children use cultural family values and experiences as the context of their play. Role-playing and the use of natural objects are common aspects of their play; however, rules and formal structure are not always a priority. Winning and losing may not always be a motivating factor. Like other American children, Native children may play with Barbie dolls and Nintendo games, but their activities often have a cultural purpose. I have seen Indian children playing "powwow," lining up all their dolls to dance in the "Grand Entry." I have observed them "clamming," pretending to go down to the bay and dig for clams.

Our Native communities, children, and cultures have survived; we have learned to walk in both worlds. For some it has been more difficult, while others have gained the benefits of a blend of both cultures. Our children are often in the hands of caretakers and teachers from outside of our communities. Teachers need to see the strengths of our culture, not just its weaknesses. They need to explore different teaching methods to encourage less vocal Indian children. Most of all, they need to understand the value of play and how it helps children become productive, healthy, and happy adults. So I'd like to express a special thank you to all educators who have taken the time and made the commitment to hear the voice of our people.

Discussion questions

This case provides a context for analyzing Douglas' behavior and motivations in the depiction of American Indians in play activities for preschoolers. It is a real-life situation in which the individual characters express their rationales and conflicting points of view with candor and conviction. The incident depicted in the case presents a dilemma or conflict for readers to resolve. To do so, they must consider all points of view objectively (including Douglas'), to identify the nature of the problem and the issues involved.

This case could either be used to analyze multiple issues (such as applying theories of play and cognitive development) or to focus attention on just one of the issues involved in the situation (such as anti-bias curriculum). No matter which objectives the discussion leader chooses, the case will highlight teacher knowledge and its relationship to practice. The major task of the discussion leader will be to assist the discussants in exploring cause-and-effect relationships, such as the following:

- ▸ What should teachers know about the relationship between play and learning?

- ▸ What does research tell teachers about the way that children develop concepts about diversity, and specifically about Native Americans?

- ▸ Why is it important for teachers to examine their own beliefs, knowledge, and opinions about diversity?

- ▸ What knowledge must early childhood professionals have to make informed decisions about selecting appropriate play materials and props for their classroom?

Questions for teacher educators and supervisors

- ► How might Douglas' college instructors change their approach to multicultural education? How might they assess their students' learning in a multicultural course?
- ► Why did all the attempts to expand Douglas' knowledge and understanding of Native American people fail?
- ► What has Douglas failed to learn about three-year-olds? How is this deficit related to the play scenario described above?
- ► What should Douglas' supervisor do next?

Questions for teachers and student interns

- ► What do you know about the nature and functions of three-year-old children's play? What advice would you give Douglas about play and learning?
- ► If Douglas made a K-W-L chart, what would you suggest that he put in the "W" and the "L" columns?
- ► How can Douglas learn about culturally diverse people who are physically removed from him or who are not visible members of his society?

Suggested readings and resources

Children's books about contemporary Native American life

King, S. (1993). *Shannon: An Ojibway dancer.* Minneapolis: Lerner.

Peters, R. M. (1992). *Clambake: A Wampanoag tradition.* Minneapolis: Lerner.

Regguinti, G. (1992). *The sacred harvest: Ojibway wild rice gathering.* Minneapolis: Lerner.

Wittstock, L. W. (1993). *Ininatig's gift of sugar: Traditional Native sugarmaking.* Minneapolis: Lerner.

Chapter 6

"Eenie, Meenie, Mynie Mo"
The Persistence of Racial Definitions in Play

Shirley Malone-Fenner, Wheelock College

Introduction

Play creates a zone of proximal development in the child. In play, the child always behaves beyond his average age, above his daily behavior; in play it is as though he were a head taller than himself. As in the focus of a magnifying glass, play contains all developmental tendencies in a condensed form and is itself a major source of development. (Vygotsky, 1978, p. 102)

This chapter will present a case that explores play in an inclusive setting. The case is a painful reminder of how powerful the dynamics of play can be. It shows how negative racial stereotypes are passed down in play and embellished by subsequent generations. The experiences described in this case provide us with anecdotal evidence reflecting traditional messages that are still prevalent today. I played this game myself as a child; my reflections on that experience and my observations of the game as an adult have raised some painful memories.

The Prison Game is a popular activity among the fourth- and fifth-graders at the elementary school discussed in this case. The game was described in a book (400 Games for School, Home, and Playground, by Ethel Acker) that was published in 1923. In this game, there are two teams. Most of the playground is neutral territory, and the two teams have home bases at each end of that territory. Next to each home base is another area for that team's "prison." The game requires the players to choose captains, prison guards, and initial prisoners. The traditional way to select these players is by repeating a rhyme. In the version of the game described here, the players use the following rhyme:

> Eenie, Meenie, Mynie Mo,
> Catch a nigger by the toe,
> If he hollers, let him go,
> Eenie, Meenie, Mynie Mo.

In the fall of 1997, I spent a day visiting the Virginia elementary school described in this case, interacting with the teachers and observing changes in their teaching techniques. During recess, I saw the fourth-graders playing an informal game that they called "Prison." I was surprised to discover that this was the same game that I had played as a child. As I watched them, vivid memories of my own unpleasant experiences with the game began to emerge. I remembered, as if it were yesterday, the prisoners, the racial slurs, and how demeaning the game felt. After all these years, this game was still being played—truly, the past remains the present!

This case raises issues of racial identity, self-esteem, the value of play, and teacher attitudes. The description of the case is followed by an analysis of the issues in the case and a series of discussion questions.

Cases can be part of an active learning strategy that helps students practice and apply their critical thinking processes by composing, interpreting, and responding to complex issues (Johannessen, 2000). Students can use the case presented here to practice their knowledge and skills and receive immediate feedback about their performance. This process can also help students address racism and other multicultural issues.

The Prison Game

The two fourth-grade classes rush eagerly out of the school door onto a fenced-in playground area—their teachers, Brenda James and Jane Parker, can barely contain them. Tom calls out, "Who wants to play Prison?" "I do!" "I do!" several children respond. Brenda looks sharply at Tom and two other boys and says, "It's okay to play the game, but no hard hitting." Jane rolls her eyes at Brenda and frowns, but says nothing.

Brenda James' class consists of twenty-one children—fifteen white, three biracial, and five black. Jane Parker's class consists of nineteen white children. The two classes usually have recess together. During playground duty, the teachers' usual practice is to observe and let the children do pretty much what they want. However, when an argument erupts between the children, Jane will usually try to stop it, while Brenda prefers to let them argue it out themselves. There have been many times when Jane has stood by reluctantly, watching sparks fly.

"We can't let them play that horrible game, Brenda," Jane says finally. "You know how out of hand they can get."

"Jane, you never want them to play anything involving running, chasing, or touching," Brenda responds. "These kids need to learn to play together."

On the playground, about thirty children are now surrounding Tom (who's white) and two other boys. Tom yells, "Line up!" Then, beginning with the first child, he goes down the line, repeating loudly:

> Eenie, Meenie, Mynie Mo,
> Catch a nigger by the toe,
> If he hollers, let him go,
> Eenie, Meenie, Mynie Mo.

All the children whom Tom is pointing to when he says "nigger" become prisoners, and those he is pointing to when he says "Mo" become prison guards or team captains. The prisoners consist of three black children—Mary, Ashley, and Ricky—and four white children—Justin, Jean, Adam, and Raymond. (It's unusual to see white children playing prisoners; when I played the game as a child, only the black children were prisoners.) The prison guards are John and Matthew (who are both white); the team captains are Ray and Cory (who are also white).

John escorts Mary, Ashley, Adam, and Justin to team A's prison, while Matt escorts Ricky, Jean, and Ray to team B's prison. As they're walking, Ricky, a black child, protests, "Why am I always one of the prisoners?" Matt yells, "Shut up, Ricky. You know you are a nigger." Ricky stares at Matt, but continues to walk quietly toward the designated prison area.

Jane Parker, who is standing nearby, begins describing the children to me. Matt heads her list of troublemakers; he's usually loud and uncontrollable. When something doesn't go his way, he will explode. Ricky is very sensitive and will do just about anything to "belong." Jane is sure that Ricky's parents would be upset if they knew that the children were playing this game and that their teachers were condoning it.

Carl, a member of team A, ventures into neutral territory to try to rescue the prisoners held by team B. Ray, the captain of team B, selects James to go after Carl. If James succeeds in catching Carl, he'll take Carl to team B's prison. Meanwhile, Cory, the captain of team A, sends another player after James; if James is caught, he will go to team A's prison.

The game continues along these lines. The last player to leave home base can capture any other player, but no player can capture any other player who left home later than he or she did. Any player can attempt to rescue a fellow team member. A player can be tagged on the way to the prison, but neither the player nor the prisoners can be tagged on their return to home base. Whenever a player is caught, or a prisoner is rescued, all the players return to their home bases. The side that has the greatest number of prisoners at the end of game is the winner.

Ways to discuss the case

On the surface, the problem depicted in this case may seem obvious. However, the solution to that problem is not as obvious. We must consider, "Who bears the ultimate responsibility for this game? The teachers? The children? The system? How might the teachers' actions (or lack of action) be exacerbating this situation?"

The issues raised by this case include racial identity, teacher attitudes and expectations, peer relationships, self-esteem, and the value and importance of play. Since the case is written from one observer's point of view, it depicts the children's play and teachers' responses from an observer's perspective. The description and the value judgments in the case are the observer's. What are the implications of these value judgments?

There are two main goals for using this case for teaching purposes. The first is to encourage students to identify and resolve the central issues raised in the case. To some degree, the specific issues that are identified may depend on the students' field of study; others are clearly associated with larger societal issues. The second goal is to explore the different ways that this case may be resolved, by using different principles and theories to analyze the facts of the case. The group's collective knowledge of play, child development, race, racism, and conflict resolution will determine how students will resolve the issues presented in the case.

During the discussion, the facilitator should help the students understand all the issues and perspectives involved in the case. The objective of the first part of the discussion might be to analyze the children's experiences. The second part of the discussion might explore what can or should be done and what effect these changes might have on the children.

This part of the discussion could begin by deciding how children's play is defined: Is it culturally defined, valued, and interpreted? Is it culturally specific? The discussion of long-term solutions and implications for the children's development will depend to some degree on the background that the participants bring to the discussion.

The heterogeneity of one of the classes described in "The Prison Game" can serve as a departure point for discussing diverse classrooms. Some of the children in this case are dealing with issues of identity, peer relationships, and self-esteem. Students can analyze the implications of the behavior of both the children and the teachers, and then share and discuss their ideas in more detail, seeking to identify both the strengths and the weaknesses of their proposed solutions.

Before the discussion

Although students may be eager to start discussing the case, the facilitator may wish to first assign groups of students to present the perspective of various social institutions. This gives students the opportunity to examine and present positions that may be contrary to their own beliefs. This is important because students usually only receive external dissent in the form of another person's opinion.

The negotiations for this case are complex and will be most meaningful if students have some experience with conflict resolution. You might wish to have students write a brief summary of a negotiation in which they have participated or are about to participate.

The facilitator should present the students with the information, analytic tools, and behavioral guidelines they will need to complete the analysis. Depending on the discipline, supplemental readings can be used (such as texts on conflict resolution).

The facilitator might start the discussion by asking students to identify the main issues raised by this case, and then to try to separate their own interests (goals and needs) from their positions.

Discussion questions
The teachers' roles

- What are Brenda's and Jane's strengths?
- Describe each teacher's attitude toward the children.

- How would you describe each teacher's style with the students?
- Can you identify each teacher's objectives?
- Are Brenda and Jane good teachers? Give examples to support your position.
- How well did Brenda and Jane handle this situation? Describe their management skills.
- What do you like about the way Brenda and Jane handled the situation?
- What factors are influencing their decisions?
- What are Brenda's weaknesses as a teacher?
- In what areas could she improve? Why? Give examples.
- What educational theories is she failing to apply, or applying inconsistently?
- What are Jane's weaknesses as a teacher?
- In what areas could she improve? Why? Give examples.
- What educational theories is she failing to apply, or applying inconsistently?

The children's behavior

- Describe the behavior of the children as a group and the behavior of individual children.
- What is the gender and racial composition of this group?
- What roles do the children play?
- Can you make any inferences about the players' personalities? What are their issues?

Analyzing and resolving the case

- Describe how the issues of racial identity, peer relationships, and the role of play are raised in this case.
- Should the teachers address these issues?
- What are the consequences of addressing (or not addressing) these issues?
- Describe the issues that this case raises, both from your perspective and from Jane's perspective, and discuss their causes.
- How should this play situation be changed?
- How can the teachers change the atmosphere on the playground?

- How can they change the atmosphere in the classroom?
- What should be done to motivate the students to change? Who should do this?
- Should more rules and procedures be imposed on the children?
- What should be done in the short term to deal with the way some of the children are being treated?
- What should be done in the longer term?

Additional discussion questions

The following questions can be used either in the group discussion of the case, or as assignment questions:

- What are the rules that children use to play games?
- Whose responsibility is it to teach children to be aware, to care, and to act appropriately?
- What rules of behavior are these children acting out in accordance with the social rules of their society?
- How do children negotiate and interpret play?
- How is play culturally defined? In what ways should play be culturally bound and relevant?
- Does this case reveal any deficit cultural meanings?
- Certain forms of play denote many historical implications. What are they?
- Else and Sturrock suggest that "Play increases affiliation with peers, releases tension, advances cognitive development and often provides a safe haven in which to engage in potentially dangerous behavior" (1999, p. 21). What are the implications of this statement for this case?
- According to Hudson and Thompson (1999), a child should be exposed to "challenges" on the playground, not to "risks." A challenge is defined as "an opportunity to engage in a contest of skill, strength, endurance, etc." With this statement in mind, what issues must we consider in this case?
- During the early years, children become aware of and begin to absorb socially prevailing negative stereotypes, feelings, and ideas about themselves and other people. In the primary years, their ideas go beyond the individual to include group identity. Some believe that after age nine, certain ideas and attitudes stay constant unless the child experiences a life-changing event (Derman-Sparks, 1993;

Wachtel, 1999). What are the implications of this statement for this case?

▶ Billig (1997) discusses the phrase, "I'm not prejudiced, but . . . " Are the children depicted in this case racially prejudiced? Are the teachers?

▶ The personalities of the two teachers are a complicating factor in this case. Is it good that two such different personalities coexist in an educational setting? Does this promote the welfare of the children? Do you think that although each teacher has doubts about the other, they still respect each other's skills?

▶ Since families and social relationships play a significant role in children's daily lives, how can teachers and parents broaden their understanding of this and move toward a culturally sensitive framework for understanding and defining play?

▶ Lopez (2001) discusses "naming one's reality." What is the "reality" depicted in this case? Whose reality is it?

Suggested readings and resources

Berk, L. E. (1994). Vygotsky's theory: The importance of make-believe play. *Young Children, 9,* 48–56.

Comer, J. P., & Poussaint, A. F. (1993). *Raising black children.* New York: Plume.

Cooper, R. M. (1996). The role of play in the acculturation process. In A. L. Phillips (Vol. Ed.), *Topics in early childhood education: Vol. 2. Playing for keeps: Supporting children's play* (pp. 89–98). St. Paul: Redleaf Press.

Fallon, M. (1996). Case-study teaching: A tool for training early interventionists. *Infants and Young Children, 8,* 59–62.

Fleer, M. (1996). Theories of play: Are they ethnocentric or inclusive? *Australian Journal of Early Childhood, 21* (4), 12–17.

Jambor, T. (1995, August). *Dimensions of play: Reflections and directions.* Paper presented at the International America Psychological Association World Conference, Parainen, Finland.

Lakin, M. B. (1996). The meaning of play: Perspectives from Pacific Oaks College. In A. L. Phillips (Vol. Ed.), *Topics in early childhood education: Vol. 2. Playing for keeps: Supporting children's play* (pp. 33–44). St. Paul: Redleaf Press.

Seifert, K. L., Hoffnung, R. J., & Hoffnung, M. (1997). *Lifespan development.* Boston: Houghton Mifflin.

Chapter 7

"But Are They *Learning* Anything?" African American Mothers, Their Children, and Play

Kimberly P. Williams, Erikson Institute (former)

Introduction

This chapter seeks to illustrate cultural differences in practices and beliefs about play in early childhood. The reader will be introduced to a conscientious preschool teacher, one of her students, and the child's mother. The vignette describes the explicit and implicit conflicts that often arise during the engagement in or observation of play, as a result of differences in values and beliefs about the purposes of play and its role in early childhood. These cultural misunderstandings reflect the tacit assumptions that we make about the forms of play that are appropriate for young children. It is these tacit assumptions, which we all hold, that we must examine and reflect upon if we are to understand and work with diverse populations of children and their families.

Chapter 8 of *Playing for Keeps: Supporting Children's Play* (Meier & Murrell, 1996) raises the issue of how play in culturally diverse communities may be construed by others, particularly those from different ethnic or socioeconomic backgrounds. Educators who are unfamiliar with the meanings that culturally diverse children and their families attach to play behavior often see, in children's play, evidence of "bad" play, sexist play, poor pretend play, and developmentally inappropriate play. This is particularly true when they observe parents interacting with children in the context of play. The play interaction of nonmainstream parents and their children often does not fit early childhood educators' view of "good" play. Meier and Murrell have termed this narrow view of appropriate play "cultural myopia." They argue that our understanding of children's play must include the social and cultural context within which they develop.

> The mental representations of the world that children draw upon in play are not merely internal representations of objects and relations. Children also internalize the rules, behavioral codes, and social constraints from the social and cultural contexts they grow up in. (p. 104)

This is also the case with parent-child play interaction. Parents' play behavior with their children reflects the tacit personal and cultural meanings that they attach to the activity. It is these meanings, attached to play, that the early childhood educator must learn to appreciate and understand in order to interact most effectively with culturally diverse parents and their children.

Culture is a shared system of meaning and understanding about family, rituals, behavior, activities, and modes of emotional response that are held by groups of people who share ethnicity or experiences (such as a history or religion). These understandings are often very subtle and not easily expressed. And yet when an act, a behavior, or a reaction that violates the cultural norms occurs, the relevant rule can be readily invoked. This is often true with respect to childrearing and children's activities.

It is difficult to understand the meaning that parents from other cultural and ethnic groups attach to play activities that appear to be culturally innocuous. Doesn't play mean the same things to all people, especially to those "born and reared" in this country? In fact, play has very different meanings cross-culturally. Like other forms of social interaction, play is very bounded by its cultural context. One example, which for me is very close to home, is how play is viewed in the context of African-American middle-class families. This perspective, particularly play in preschool and other early childhood programs, must be understood in the context of African-American parents' expectations of and reasons for choosing a preschool program.

My assumption is that the meaning of play is different in the African-American culture. (As Tudge and Putnam (1995) suggest, even within the

United States there is unlikely to be homogeneity across all subcultural groups or within the same cultural group across time. In this vignette, I am referring to a particular segment of African-American culture—midwestern, urban, college-educated, professionally employed, native-born black people who are not first- or second-generation immigrants of recent Caribbean descent or African descent.) For this group, the meanings and practices associated with play are intricately connected to the issues of literacy, achievement, and parenting roles. Although in the mainstream culture play may be viewed as the work of the child, in this cultural group it is inextricably connected to the parents' long-term expectations for their children.

In this chapter, I provide a vignette of a teacher-parent-child interaction around naturally occurring play in the preschool context. After the vignette I discuss the social and pretend-play activities presented and the parents' values and beliefs about social play and the preschool context. Finally, I will address the implications of this case for early childhood students and teachers and suggest some strategies for bridge building with culturally diverse parents and children.

Parents' Day at Birdsong Day School

It is Parents' Day at Birdsong Day School, a popular infant care through prekindergarten corporate preschool program housed on the seventeenth floor of the main corporate offices of a Fortune 500 company. The company, which is located in a suburb of Chicago, is popular with middle-income professional families, and its corporate preschool provides welcome relief to corporate parents who are trying to balance their careers with the needs of young children. Although parents are free to drop in anytime to see their children, few do so, except during the workday lunch hour.

Parents' Day is a twice-yearly opportunity for parents to come in to their children's classrooms and spend the day with their children. The day is preplanned by a parent-teacher committee and approved by senior management, and every effort is made by the program to accommodate a wide range of activities and special events. In the past, parents have remarked that Parents' Day really helped them understand the daily lives of their children and of their children's preschool teachers.

On this Parents' Day, Sandy Roberts, the head teacher in the three-year-old's classroom, stands at the door and greets the parents and their children as they come in. The children rush in ahead of their parents, anxious to act as tour guides and plan activities. As usual, the children bring along one or two special "home" toys. The program allows them to bring one or two toys to school daily, to help them build a bridge between their two special places. The children must take their toys home at the end of the school day.

The Birdsong parents are a little shy, but excited about the opportunity to visit their children's classrooms for an extended period. The parents of the three-year-old children greet Sandy and try to locate their children in the crowd. One parent remarks how similar all the children look in a crowd. Sandy laughs and agrees that it might seem that way at first glance.

Once most of the parents have arrived, Sandy begins to describe the day's agenda. The parents are introduced to the special play areas in the room and on the patio directly outside, in the enclosed play area. Sandy notes that parents may want to get acquainted with the pretend-play areas, including the kitchen, restaurant, living room, school, and grocery store. There are also, she suggests, a lot of opportunities to cuddle with the children in the book reading area. She announces that lunch will be in the main eating area and will be served "family-style"—bowls of food will be placed around the table, and everyone will serve themselves. After lunch, the children will take a nap. During this period, she suggests, parents may chat quietly, or they may visit the parent resource room, which has films and books on parenting issues including toilet training, feeding, discipline, divorce, and hearing and speech issues. At the end of their naptime, the children and parents will gather for a story, read by Sandy. Then it will be time to clean up and to go home.

As the day begins, the children move quickly into the various play areas with their parents. Andi, a three-year-old girl, anxiously pulls her mother toward her favorite "room." This room has lots of animals, including big teddy bears, toy animals, and an assortment of other stuffed animals. Andi loves pretending with the animals. She particularly likes Frank, a loveable, huggable bear. Andi introduces Frank to her mother and begins playing on the floor with Frank and the other animals.

Andi is Mrs. Smith's first child. Mr. and Mrs. Smith are both middle-management African-American professionals, and they waited several years before having a child. They are very anxious to provide Andi with everything she needs to grow healthy and strong. They are also very concerned that she be prepared for kindergarten.

Mrs. Smith sits on a small chair and watches Andi play with Frank. Andi begins to alternate between Frank and a red tricycle parked nearby. The tricycle is just a little too big for Andi, and her mother starts to give her step-by-step instructions for riding it. As Andi begins to gain confidence, she pulls her bear, Frank, onto the tricycle with her. Mrs. Smith watches Andi play with Frank and eventually joins her in the pretend play.

Mrs. Smith (watching Andi trying to ride her tricycle): "You pedal it. Frank the bear knows how to ride. Do you want to give Frank a ride?"

Andi tries to put Frank on the tricycle with her.

Mrs. Smith (to an observer): "Frank's been with her a long time."

After unsuccessfully trying to simultaneously steer the tricycle and hold on to Frank, Andi eventually opts to leave him behind.

Andi: "Frank, I gotta go."

Mrs. Smith: "Sorry, Frank."

Later, Andi places Frank in front of her on the tricycle. She sits on the tricycle seat and puts both her arms around Frank, pretending that Frank is riding her on the tricycle. Her mother clearly enjoys watching Andi play. She joins in by giving Andi a suggestion for handling Frank and simultaneously riding the tricycle.

Sandy, who has been walking around the room observing her students playing with their parents, now stops to watch Andi, Frank, and Mrs. Smith. Sandy suggests to Mrs. Smith that she sit on the floor and play with Andi. She suggests that Mrs. Smith might want to ride the tricycle while holding Frank, so that she might be even more engaged in Andi's pretend play. Mrs. Smith declines the suggestion and continues to talk to Andi about the way she is playing with Frank.

Andi (to an observer): "This is mine. That's mine. Frank is taking me for a ride."

Mrs. Smith: "You stand up. You have to stand up on the back and Frank will give you a ride."

Frank is unsuccessful in steering the tricycle and is deposited on the rug. Andi continues to ride her bicycle in the play area.

Andi and her mother eventually grow tired of the animal play area. They decide to go into the household area. This "room" is well stocked with a sofa, a toy washing machine and dryer, a vacuum cleaner, a table with four pint-sized chairs, and a kitchen containing a stove and refrigerator. There are also cabinets with facsimile food in cans and boxes. One corner of the "room" holds a toy computer, a cassette tape player, and a toy CD player.

Andi immediately walks over to the cabinets and, from a lower shelf, pulls out some baby powder that has been placed there by mistake. She directs her mother's attention to the baby powder, which she calls "Carpet Fresh," and begins to sprinkle it on the carpet. Andi's mother tries to discourage her daughter from sprinkling the "Carpet Fresh" all over the carpet. She doesn't want to discourage Andi's play, but also doesn't want her to spread baby powder all over the carpet.

Andi: "Look."

Mrs. Smith: "What do you have?"

Andi (shaking powder): "You clean up. You use the powder to clean up the room."

Mrs. Smith: "Use the powder to clean up the room?"

Andi: "Um-hmmm. Look, this is the fresh. This is the powder to clean up the room."

Mrs. Smith: "That's not Carpet Fresh, that's the [baby] powder for you. If you put Carpet Fresh on it, then what do you do to it?"

Andi (vacuuming): "You clean it. Put your feet up. Put your feet on the couch."

Mrs. Smith: "I have shoes on. I'll get the couch dirty."

Andi: "Oh. I've got super powder. Me."

Mrs. Smith (noticing that the powder is spraying on the rug): "Hey, hey, that really is open. Thank you."

Andi: "This is fresh for dinner."

Mrs. Smith: "Andi, no, give me the big powder. (Mrs. Smith closes the top of the powder.) There, now you can shake it. Andi, this powder is . . . you have enough powder, now you need to vacuum it up (pointing to the toy vacuum cleaner). Put that powder back."

Andi: "No, I want it."

Mrs. Smith: "What are you going to do with it?"

Andi: "Put some more on it."

Mrs. Smith: "Okay. Don't open the powder, okay? Andi? Don't open the powder. Vacuum it up like mommy does. Why don't you put the powder back on the table?"

Andi: "No."

Mrs. Smith: "Please?"

Andi: "No."

Andi's mother is unable to distract her through another reality-based pretend play role: vacuuming up the "Carpet Fresh." However, a few moments later Andi is distracted by the music of a cassette tape that her mother has strategically turned on, and she begins to dance and sing. She puts "Carpet Fresh" down and her mother removes it from view.

Andi sits on the carpet and begins rocking her home toy "Baby Sally" to sleep. She often rocks "Baby Sally" in the rocking chair in the corner of the household room. Mrs. Smith watches Andi play with Baby Sally.

Andi (to Baby Sally): "Time for night-night."

Mrs. Smith: "Time for Sally to go night-night?"

Andi: "Um hum. Where's the rocking chair?"

Mrs. Smith: "Where's the rocking chair? There it is. Do you want to bring the rocking chair out?"

Andi: "Um hum. Rock-a-bye baby. Shhhhh. Rock-a-bye baby in the tree tops."

Mrs. Smith: "When the bough breaks."

Andi (singing): "And the cradle will fall."

Mrs. Smith (singing with Andi): "And down will come Sally, cradle and all."

Andi (to Baby Sally): "Let's get some milk for you."

Mrs. Smith: "Okay. Got your fresh milk?"

Andi: "A fresh milk bottle."

Mrs. Smith: "Why don't you sit in your chair or sit at the table and feed her. That will be a lot easier. You know how mommy sits at the table when she feeds you? That's how you feed your babies."

Andi: "I don't want to."

Mrs. Smith: "Why do you want to sit on the box? You can't feed Sally if you're sitting on the box. You've got to go sit at the table to feed her, because you can't hold her. You don't feed your babies on the floor; you have to hold them. I guess this works for you, huh? I guess you say 'whatever works, mommy, she's eating, isn't she?'"

Sandy walks into the room and compliments Andi on how well she's taking care of Baby Sally. She comments to Mrs. Smith that part of the learning in pretending is in doing things in fun and new ways. Mrs. Smith disagrees and notes that Andi should not eat on the floor or put food, pretend or not, on or near the floor. Andi continues to play with Baby Sally. She takes her bowl to the play kitchen and pretends to get more food for the baby.

Andi: "I'm getting some more."
Mrs. Smith: "What is she eating?"
Andi: "Some Cream of Wheat cereal."
Mrs. Smith: "Okay, got some more?"
Andi: "I'm feeding her more now."
Mrs. Smith: "That's fine. I still say you'd do better at the table."

After this, Andi and her mom continue to play in the household area and enjoy the remainder of their morning.

Analysis

Andi lives in a stable home that abounds in books and toys. As an only child, she has experienced a great deal of attention. As Levine (1980) has suggested, certain groups of Western parents have invested a great deal in their children's upbringing. The hopes and dreams of the family's future rest in these children. As African-American middle-class children, they carry the additional burden and culturally perceived responsibility of being double minorities: both relatively advantaged, and black.

Black middle-class parents do not take education acquisition for granted. They begin the process of educating their children in the very young preschool years and consider it a responsibility to have their children "ready" for preschool and kindergarten. To them, this means that the children are equipped with the ability to count and recognize alphabet letters, a relatively large expressive and receptive vocabulary, and general behavior management skills. When asked, they express a desire for preschools that offer opportunities for socialization and social play. Yet when they elaborate on their ideal preschool visions, academic expectations repeatedly come to the fore (Williams, 1994). For these parents, play and socialization are the work of the parent.

Finding the right combination of academics and socialization is a concern frequently expressed by African-American middle-class parents. These parents want their children to develop social skills in the preschool years and yet are extremely concerned about the very concrete and visible development of pre-academic skills. They are very concerned that their children will be "ready" for kindergarten. By this, they typically mean that their children will be able to read or demonstrate reading readiness skills; write their names; count; and expressively and receptively identify colors and the alphabet.

There are four points that can help mainstream early childhood teachers understand the difference between their views of developmentally appropriate play and African-American middle-class parents' desire to balance early literacy acquisition and social needs:

▸ Teachers should be aware that many black middle-class parents view early literacy and reading readiness skills as deliberately and didactically taught, rather than naturally acquired and without direct guidance through play experiences. They consider these skills to be important both for preschool preparedness and later academic success.

▸ In African-American middle-class families, parent-child social play at home is often literacy-based and goal-directed, both in content and structure. For example, parents encourage children to combine social pretend play with early literacy (such as playing store or school).

▸ In these families, pretend play may be less child directed.

▸ The pretend play between parent (usually the mother) and child is typically used by the mothers as an opportunity for socialization of cultural practices and is didactically jointly constructed.

African-American middle-class parents' beliefs about play can contribute to differences in structure and content in their engagement in parent-child play. This play often looks more structured and didactic than the play described in the mainstream literature, because it serves specific cultural and social purposes.

For middle-class black parents, play offers an opportunity to instruct the child in pre-academic skills. Play, and particularly parental engagement in play, serves as the context for learning. Children are taught the alphabet, vocabulary words covering many topics, and counting. They are also implicitly—and on occasion explicitly—taught to listen to and follow instructions. In this case, Andi's mother tried to teach Andi to follow directions in the context of her play activities, for example, by instructing Andi to stand up and then ride Frank. She allowed little, if any, sustained self-directed play.

Pretend play also offers the parents an opportunity to teach valued social skills. During ethnographic interviews, Fung (1994) found that Taiwanese mothers discussed the importance of "opportunity education" —of using children's everyday activities and ongoing interactions as a context for instruction, which they contrasted with ineffective "lecturing" to young children. Andi's mother moves in and out of pretend-play contexts in order to teach valuable lessons about home care, self-care, and care of others.

For example, when Andi's mother joined in the "feeding Baby Sally" pretend play with her daughter, she attempted to jointly construct, with Andi, her expert-versus-novice (Vygotsky, 1978) view of the rules of behavior for feeding a baby. Mrs. Smith believed that proper feeding techniques included sitting at a table. She joined in the pretend play, but found it necessary to invoke sociocultural rules about appropriate behavior. A mild conflict ensued while Andi's mother remained within the pretend-play mode. Andi continued to sit on the floor while feeding her baby and her mother ended both her participation in the pretend play and her discussion of Andi's method of feeding the baby. During the feeding activity, Andi clearly demonstrated pretend-play behavior. She transformed objects (such as Sally's bottle) and incorporated pretend ideas into her play scenario.

Andi's mother alternated between engaging in pretend play with her daughter and directing Andi's pretend play from outside the activity (as in the episode involving the tricycle and the bear). This form of engagement, stage management, is also a characteristic of play between parents and children. When parents stage-manage play, they attempt to direct the content and the story line. African-American middle-class parents may engage in stage management in an effort to practice "opportunity education." The child continues to play while being taught valued skills and behaviors.

Sandy (the preschool teacher) was concerned about the mother's lack of embeddedness in her child's play. She suggested that Mrs. Smith become more involved in Andi's pretend play by sitting on the carpet and embedding herself in Andi's story. Andi's mother demurred, because she did not see that as the role of an adult. She preferred to stage-manage her daughter's play activity, so that Andi would understand how to "do it the right way" in the real world. To this end, she did not want Andi to feed Baby Sally while sitting on the carpet. In her view, Andi must learn the proper way to feed a baby, and play will be the vehicle for this learning.

Bridging different views of play

For the early childhood professional, building bridges from the teacher to the parent is an essential step in the creation of positive, successful, and sustained home and school relationships. Every day, the early childhood teacher attempts to create a classroom environment that supports social, physical, and emotional development, while providing support for cognitive development through developmentally appropriate activities. This is a challenge even when both teacher and parents are from the same culture. It is even more difficult when the teacher does not understand the parents' cultural values and beliefs, or how those views relate to the parents' interpretation of the importance of, emphasis on, and appropriate structure for the two primary experiences that define preschool experiences: social play and pretend play.

Therefore, the early childhood teacher has a responsibility to build a bridge to the parents' beliefs. This bridge must be rooted in an appreciation of other cultural beliefs and practices. In addition, the teacher must look with "wise eyes" at the play of African-American and other minority children. She must consider the content of the children's play and reflect on how it may be related to home and out-of-school social experiences. In doing so, she should examine her own theories of how preliteracy skills emerge during play and consider weaving those skills into the content of her students' self-directed, naturally occurring play.

To bridge the gap between her perspective and that of Mrs. Smith, Sandy might consider developing a pretend-play portfolio for Andi. She could periodically observe Andi engaging in pretend play (either alone or with classmates). She could note the play content or theme and Andi's play behavior, including the richness of the pretend play and the social, emotional, physical, and cognitive skills that are emerging in it. She might also note the developmental goals that are being supported as Andi develops her skills during play. Three to four times a year, she could send the play portfolio home and ask Mrs. Smith to add her own comments, such as the pretend-play themes that she's seen Andi engaging in at home. This might encourage Mrs. Smith to consider the value of less-directed pretend play in Andi's development.

There is no one best way for children to play. When parents' and teachers' views of play are in conflict, the teacher must communicate with the parents about the kind of play that their children engage in at school and at home. There should be a frank discussion about the blend of cognitive and social-emotional skills within play contexts. The teacher should assure the parents that spontaneous literacy-based play will not be discouraged in the classroom.

The early childhood professional must also consider the structure of the children's play and how the toys they play with may discourage or encourage self-directed pretend play. She must be willing to engage parents in conversations and small-group discussions, perhaps during parent group meetings, about how the toys might encourage self-directed pretend play that also supports early literacy. Honest conversations about the similarities and differences in home and school play structure will solidify the bridge.

Finally, the early childhood professional must be prepared with concrete examples for parents regarding the development of cognition within play contexts. It can be frustrating and demeaning for parents to be told that their children are learning, when parents only see their children engaging in social and pretend play without specific parallels to reading, numeracy, following directions, or the development of receptive and expressive vocabulary.

Black middle-class parents often believe that their children must be prepared to excel academically. They must feel reassured that their children will be ready and able to meet the challenges that lie ahead in elementary school. Given the recent push, in many cities, for accountability in standardized test performance, and the trend in pedagogy toward direct instruction in the primary grades, these parents must be given examples of concrete linkages between the value of play and pre-academic development.

Like their children's teachers, African-American parents want their children to be well-rounded and socially and cognitively prepared to be both productive future members of the larger society and well-functioning representatives of their cultural group.

Discussion questions
Questions for teachers

- How can you, as an early childhood teacher, help parents such as Andi's mother see the long-term benefits of play as learning?
- What problem(s) was Andi working on in her play with Baby Sally and Frank the bear? How could that learning be supported in a preschool program?
- What meaning did Andi seem to ascribe to her pretend play with her doll, Baby Sally?

▶ How could you design play opportunities that would culturally fit the interests of each individual child? How could you find out about the home and social lives of the children in your preschool classroom?

Projects and Activities

▶ Ask parents to allow you to observe them playing in their homes with their children (or ask them to bring in a short videotape of parent-child play time experiences). What activities do they view as play? What is the content of the play? What types of toys do they use? How does the parent participate in the play experience?

▶ Review the examples of Andi's play. Look for instances of dynamic knowledge construction versus repetition and imitation.

▶ Identify examples of parental use of opportunity education during parent-child play.

Further discussion

▶ How could pretend play with potentially pre-academic overtones (for example, library, grocery store, Sunday school, and school) support general preliteracy and reading-readiness skills without direct guidance or didactic instruction? Plan these activities and consider your role in them as an early childhood teacher.

Suggested readings and resources

Garvey, C. (1990). *Play: The developing child series.* Cambridge, MA: Harvard University Press.

Haight, W., & Miller, P. (1993). *Pretending at home: Early development in a sociocultural context.* New York: State University of New York Press.

Williams, K. (1991). Storytelling as a bridge to literacy. *The Journal of Negro Education, 60* (3).

Chapter 8

The Welcoming Place
Tungasuvvingat Inuit Head Start Program

Gretchen Reynolds, Bank Street College (former)

Introduction

I'm not surprised by a recent report suggesting that Canadian college students in early childhood education are not well prepared to work with diverse populations upon graduation (Bernhard et al., 1997). As a teacher-educator in early childhood education at Algonquin College in Ottawa, I hope that our students will demonstrate respect and appreciation for cultural and linguistic diversity, a willingness to examine their own biases, collaborative approaches to working with others, and competency in practices that empower children and parents. However, I'm aware that we do not accomplish all that we might wish, and I make a personal commitment to deepen my own understanding of the educational approaches that value and promote diversity. One of the ways I can do this is to observe early childhood programs in the local community and to tell the stories of my visits.

One question that I would like to answer is how play can have a role in scaffolding children's cultural understanding. The role of play in young children's learning has been widely documented and advocated. Bredekamp and Copple (1997) note that

> Teachers stimulate and support children's engagement in play and child-chosen activities. Teachers extend the child's thinking and learning within

these child-initiated activities by posing problems, asking questions, making suggestions, adding complexity to tasks, and providing information, materials, and assistance as needed to enable a child to consolidate learning and move to the next level of functioning. (p. 128)

As we have written elsewhere (Jones & Reynolds, 1992) there is also value in children's cooperative dramatic (pretend) play. For children ages three to five, becoming a master player is the height of developmental achievement. Master players are skilled at representing their experiences symbolically in self-initiated improvisational drama. Sometimes alone, sometimes in collaboration with others, they play out their fantasies and the events of their daily lives. Through pretend play, young children consolidate their understanding of the world, their language, and their social skills. The skillful teacher of young children makes such play possible and helps children to continue to improve it.

This leads me to wonder whether children can also learn about culture through play, and what the teacher's role in this would be. The case described below explores how teachers in a Head Start facility for urban Inuit children are using a rich environment, thoughtful teaching interventions, and quality play to cultivate children's knowledge of their Inuit roots.

Lakin (1996) describes one theory of the possibility of using play as a context for the young child to learn about community. She quotes John Nimmo, a faculty member at Pacific Oaks College, who has been exploring the theory that "play is a significant context for both developing and revealing a child's sense of community" (p. 38). In a course that John teaches about community, students explore a variety of questions: What is the role of play in acquiring a sense of community belonging? In what ways does a child's play reflect her understanding of community? How do children play in their own neighborhood/cultural communities? How does this relate to play in school contexts?

Tungasuvvingat Inuit Head Start Program

The Tungasuvvingat Inuit Head Start Program in Ottawa had been open for more than a year at the time of my visit. Funded by Health Canada under the Aboriginal Head Start Initiative, the program's purpose is to "enhance the overall development of Inuit preschool children; foster positive parenting through support and education; and promote the retention of the Inuit culture and language" (Tungasuvvingat Inuit Head Start Program, 1997). The handbook states its policy of emphasizing Inuit culture and language:

> The retention of the Inuit culture and language is paramount in this program. Curriculum activities and materials should reflect the Inuit culture whenever possible. Inuktitut will be considered an official language of the program and will be promoted throughout all activities during the day. It is also the policy of the program to employ Inuit staff as much as possible. (p. 2)

The Inuit were formerly called "Eskimo" people. They traditionally live in the Arctic regions, although many Inuit now live in urban communities in Canada. There are approximately five hundred Inuit living in Ottawa, a large industrialized city thousands of miles from the environment to which their culture is indigenous. Some of the children's parents have grown up in urban areas, after their parents relocated to the south. In Canada, fluency in English or French is necessary for survival, and several parents have lost the ability to speak Inuktitut, their native language. The Head Start parents want their children's early education to emphasize Inuit culture and language. They don't want to lose their culture, and they believe that this program is a good beginning for their children. As Liz Lightford, the program coordinator at the time of my visit, told me,

> I think being in the South is a heartache for some parents. For Inuit, family is important to them, and home is important. So when they're away from home, even though they choose to be in Ottawa, the homesickness that they feel is a real heartache. So they want their kids to have some of home in the city, and it's a way of passing on themselves through their kids, even though the children can't be in the North, learning it traditionally. (personal communication, 1997)

Tungasuvvingat means "welcoming place," and this is a place where I, a cultural outsider, always feel welcome. I'm invited to visit, which I do often, to see the program, the children, and teachers in action.

The Play Environment

The environment of the center is familiar to an early childhood educator. There are blocks, Lego building blocks, puzzles, writing and drawing supplies, and a wheelchair for dolls. The new computer is very popular, whether for one child or for two children working cooperatively. Elaine, a teacher, tells me that Inuktitut software for learning both the written and spoken language will soon be published.

My eye is attracted to the array of materials and objects that suggest northern themes or are used by Inuit people. The book corner contains a shelf filled with children's books in Inuktitut (a few with English translations) and stuffed animals commonly found in the Arctic. Dulled *ulus* (women's knives) are available at the playdough table. In the block corner, a child is playing with several miniature rubber seals, a dolphin, and a whale, which she has carefully arranged on a child-sized *kamutiik* (Arctic sled) and is pulling across the room. In the dramatic play area, I see dolls with brown skin, dark hair, and dark eyes, a child-sized *amauti* (a traditional baby-carrying parka), *kamiik* (Inuit books), and caribou skins. In the music corner, the children can play Inuit drums or listen to *aiyaya* songs or throat-singing on tape. Inuktitut syllabics decorate the walls and a big set of colorful homemade alphabet blocks. The children's cubbies show their names in both Inuktitut and English. A water table contains pebbles, a rubber sea turtle and dolphins, and several large clamshells.

The Bone Game

A sheet is spread out on the floor. Accompanied by several children, Ina Kuluguqtuq settles down with some things in a plastic grocery bag. Ina is the children's Inuk teacher; her first language is Inuktitut. She was raised in Pangnirtung, Northwest Territories. In an earlier conversation, she told me, "We were living in outpost camp. Mom and Dad were my teachers. Everything I know today they're from my mom and dad, and grandma." When she was fourteen years old, Ina started attending a settlement school, where she learned English. "It was hard, because I didn't speak English in those days. I found it very hard, but gradually I learned." In 1982 she went to Iqaluit for teacher training through McGill University's Eastern Arctic Teacher Education Program. "I got a job right away in Iqaluit; a job was waiting for me. I was a kindergarten teacher in a public school for three years, then grade two. All the children were Inuit. All the teaching was in Inuktitut, we used no English at all" (personal communication, 1997).

By now, eight or nine children have gathered on the rug in front of Ina, who is holding a small blue-and-white crocheted bag in her lap. "This was my favorite game when I was a little girl," she says. She ties a long piece of nylon rope to form a loop at one end, and pokes the open loop into the bag. Then she pulls the drawstring, closing the bag tight. Invoking a ritual, she shakes the bag, saying, "Sha la la la la la!" The children watch, fascinated. Then she hitches the nylon rope tight and pulls out a handful of small bones that have been caught in the loop.

"Let's see what kind of friends I got!" Ina says, separating the stones and naming them one by one, according to size. "I have *anaana* (mom). I have *panik* (girl). I have another girl. And this is *ataata* (dad). Three girls, a baby, mom, and an *ataata*." All the children are eager to have a turn. They wait patiently as Ina gives each of them a chance to play the bone game. Whenever someone shakes the crocheted bag, children merrily join the incantation, "Sha la la la la la!" Eventually their energy for the bone game wanes, but Ina leaves it out for them to play with during the morning.

Some time later, a child sits down and begins putting the bones into the crocheted bag. In response to her call, "Help me," the other aboriginal teacher, Elaine Shipley, a Swampy Cree from Peter Ballentyne Cree Nation in northern Saskatchewan, moves over. Another child, Bianca, joins them, on her tummy, watching.

Elaine counts, "One, two, three-four-five," as the first child places the bones inside the bag. Holding a bone up, she says, "That's my daddy."

Elaine asks, "Where is your *anaana?*"

"Right here, my *anaana!*" the child answers. Bianca begins picking up bones too, and the two girls put them into the bag together.

Christina approaches. She watches as Elaine picks up a doll and rocks it lovingly. A second child reaches out her arms, and Elaine hands her the doll, as she would a baby. The child cradles the doll, kisses it, and hands it back to Elaine. Elaine suggests, "Let's give her a bath." She brings over a plastic tub and sits the doll in it, with two bottles in case of hunger. Meanwhile, Christina has pulled an *amauti* over her head. Taking the doll from the bathtub, she asks Elaine to tuck the baby into the carrying pouch on the back of the *amauti*. For a long time afterward, Christina carries the doll around with her. Many of the Head Start mothers proudly choose this baby-carrying method.

Four Markers

I'm fascinated by an example of hostile reciprocity (Prescott et al., 1975). At the white board, two girls disagree over the possession and control of the four available markers. A student teacher, Lisa (a Micmac—an Indian tribe indigenous to Nova Scotia and New Brunswick), comes over to point out the inequity of their holdings: one person has three markers and the other person has one. Which is more?

Lisa steps aside, and the dispute continues, with one child withholding and the other complaining. The child who had the three markers leaves briefly. They are snatched up by the other child until she returns, when the dispute starts all over again. Chuckling to myself as the sparring continues, I think, "What a normal, natural way for young children to figure out issues of sharing, negotiation, and fairness." If Lisa had imposed a solution on them, the girls would have been deprived of the discomfort of conflict.

The Fish Camp

Taking my hand, four-year-old Christian guides me over to a child-sized table in front of a large, bright window. "Let's play here," he says eagerly. His invitation to play with the miniature people is a greeting I warmly accept—I'm curious about this particular set of toys and how a young Inuit child would use them.

The miniature figures have been invitingly arranged on the small table. There are four adults—two females and two males—with light brown skin and dark hair. I notice that the women figures are wearing pants. The adults are sitting together inside a simple, open-sided building. There are also two babies in cribs. Among the other accessories are two small tents, several coniferous trees, and few smaller outbuildings. Does this setting suggest life in the North to the children, I wonder? It certainly doesn't look like a city scene.

I wonder if Christian's dramatic play will reflect what he knows about the Inuit lifestyle in the North. A young child's play often reflects everyday life events, and Christian's daily experiences are situated in downtown Ottawa. Christian's Inuk dad has been to the North, but Christian has never been there. As Christian and I play, I remember to turn on my tape recorder. Here are some excerpts from our play dialogue:

Christian tells me that the family is waking up to fish for breakfast. Holding one of the women figures, I ask him, "Are you hungry, Daddy? We're going to have fish for breakfast."

Ina is working in the nearby art area with some other children. Overhearing our play, she calls out, "Christian, what's *fish* in Inuktitut?"

Without hesitating, Christian answers, "*Iqaluk!*"

Ina: "Right! You tell her!"

Christian (turning to me): *"Iqaluk!"* Indicating a wooden figurine, he says, "Pretend this is *iqaluk!*"

We invent a cooking place—the slanted top of one of the cribs. I say *"Iqaluk,* stay there and cook." Christian repeats, "Hey, stay there, *iqaluk,* and cook!"

Christian puts one of the men into a tent and makes an alternating breathing and light snoring sound. He sings sweetly, "Rock-a-bye baby on the tree top, when the wind blows the cradle will rock. Rock-a-bye-baby!"

Me: "What's the daddy doing?"

Christian: "He's sleeping now."

Me: "Is the fish cooking?"

Christian: "No, it's still alive. It's not cooking. It's going to bite you!"

Me: "Why are you biting me, fish? Daddy, how do we kill the fish so we can cook it for breakfast?"

Christian: "We cut it with the knife. Cut! I cutted it."

Me: "How did you cut it?"

Christian: "With a big knife."

Me: "That means the fish is going to be ready for breakfast." After a pause, I ask, "Daddy, what do you have to do today?"

Christian: "Let's go for a walk and see fireworks! Yahoo! Let's go!"

Me: "Out here on the ice where the fish are?"

Christian: "Yeah, I see it!"

Me: "You're very excited, Daddy. What's happening?"

Christian (shouting, as the male figure): "Look at that one! That's a big one! That's a big dog!" Then Christian stops playing and gives me a big hug, saying, "Now you be the daddy, and I will be the mommy."

Building an Inukshuk

On the floor in the art area, Ina and several children are busy painting medium-sized cardboard boxes with sponges that they have dipped in black and brown paint. Walking past, Liz comments, "That's going to be a great *inukshuk!*" She sees the puzzled look on my face and points to a large painting by a community member of an *inukshuk.* It's a cairn built of rocks, resembling a human shape but taller than either of the two Inuit people who are standing upon it.

I can understand only some of Ina's conversation with the children, because she switches between Inuktitut and English. I later transcribe a small sample, which Ina translates:

"All right!"

"We can go like this."

"*Ajungi!*" (Doing good.)

"You want to do one, too?"

"Next? My friend Ariana!"

"Here's your box."

"*Atiingilirit.*" (Please sit down.)

"*Piujuq,* Christina!" (Beautiful, Christina!)

"Want some more brown?"

"*Qinitaq?*" (Black?)

"*Imaak.*" (Like this.)

"Do the other side."

"This part now."

"You're finished? *Taimaa?*" (You're finished?)

"*Takuliruk!*" (Look at it!)

"*Ajungi!*" (Doing good!)

"*Nakummiik!*" (Thank you.)

In answer to my question, "What's an *inukshuk?*" Ina replies:

There are a lot of ways you can use *inukshuk*. They can be used for when you go out hunting. If there was a really good hunting area, you put *inukshuk* with the rocks. If you're going out looking for caribou in the tundra, as you go further and further, you put small *inukshuks* so when you're going back, you'll know the trail going back home. Also they can be used for challenges, because sometimes rocks are heavier and sometimes they are lighter, and the men challenge each other. There are lots of *inukshuks* around up north. In a big tundra area, if you're looking for caribou, and you didn't find any for a couple of hours, they put an *inukshuk* and walk farther, to make sure they don't get lost coming back when it gets dark. We know when we seek the *inukshuk* that we're on the right path. (personal communication, 1997)

Several days later I return to hand out some photographs that I took at the center. I ask Ina, "What did you do with the children's painted boxes?" Smiling broadly, she says, "We made an *inukshuk*. You want to see it?"

Ina takes me out into the front entrance. The painted boxes have been assembled in the shape of an *inukshuk* that stands tall on top of the cubbies. Ina explains that there are small rocks in the blockbuilding area for making *inukshuks*, but that this one will be kept here permanently. She says, "This *inukshuk* means 'welcoming place.' We know where to go.

That's our *inukshuk* in here, and we know where to go. We won't get lost in here."

Inuit Culture Makes This School a Community

My documentation of the play at the Tungasuvvingat Inuit Head Start Program is a small window on the many things that Inuit children are learning about their indigenous culture. Their curiosity is stimulated by an environment that contains an array of strange and wonderful objects from their culture, and other toys suggestive of the Inuit lifestyle. The children have access to people who have a history of living with the objects and who want to explain and demonstrate their use.

Ina takes out a big piece of dried caribou sinew. "What is that, Ina?" the ever curious four-year-old Christian wants to know.

"It's a thread for making clothing," Ina replies. Christian watches as Ina breaks off a long, threadlike piece. She continues, "You know what, my dad used this to clean his teeth. He goes like this." Holding the thread close to her mouth, Ina makes exaggerated flossing motions. The children giggle.

Christian imitates his teacher's flossing gesture, and then asks for a try with the real thing. Ina hands him the thread, reminding him to throw it in the garbage when he's finished. Looking somewhat puzzled, but also curious and amused, Christian experiments for several minutes to work the hairy, distasteful piece of caribou sinew into the spaces between his teeth.

Ina described to me how the opportunity to work with the children and teach them the Inuit traditions was bringing back her childhood memories:

> Today when I am trying to plan, trying to think about our Inuit ways, my grandma is coming back. They (memories) are coming back to me since we started this program, gradually they're coming back. For years they've put away somewhere, years. When you love the job, they'll come back. That's happening here. When I was growing up hunting, going camping, all the Inuit lifestyle, and here I want the little ones to know it too. My grandma, every time she was doing something, cleaning fish, cleaning sealskin, cutting the meat, she would invite us to watch her, and she'd talk about it. She would invite the kids over just to watch her when she's opening the seal, and why this is good for you. That was very interesting to watch, and you believe it, because that's your grandma telling you! (personal communication, 1997)

In response to my questions about the children's understanding of Inuktitut, Ina described the effect for her in using her native language every day:

> To me, the language is everything. If I don't speak my language for about a week, let's say I speak only English, I'm craving for something, and I know exactly what I'm craving for—speaking in my mother tongue. When I speak Inuktitut I just relax again, my muscles were all uptight. It's very important, my language. It's always in me, I always speak it, especially around here, and when I see other Inuit I feel more special, especially living down South. When I'm in an English setting, I feel smaller. Especially living down here, I feel like I have two sides, one side in English, and one in Inuktitut. That's why so many of us Inuit are losing our language. When we've been down here for long we're just stuck in one, English, because we don't hear Inuktitut anymore. When I'm speaking my mother tongue I feel very strong, more comfortable, I feel good about it. (personal communication, 1997)

Some of the children's parents don't speak Inuktitut, because their parents relocated to the South. During free play, Ina uses Inuktitut comfortably and naturally. In small groups, the children learn their language in a friendly and structured environment. In that setting, Ina's approach to teaching Inuktitut is similar to methods used in ESL (English as a Second Language) programs, where the emphasis is on acquiring vocabulary. One month's theme is family, and in this excerpt from my tapes, Ina is reinforcing the names of family members:

Ina: "I need your help with our Inuktitut. What's 'mom' in Inuktitut?"
"*Anaana!*"
Ina: "What's 'dad' in Inuktitut?"
"*Ataata.*"
Ina: "What's a girl in Inuktitut?"
"A *panik.*"
Ina: "What's a boy in Inuktitut?"
"*Irnniq.*"
Ina: "What's a grandpa in Inuktitut?"
"*Ataatakiak.*"
Ina: "Grandma?"
"*Anaanasiak.*"
Ina: "Okay, can you say them all? How about dad?"
"*Ataata.*"

Ina: "How about *anaana?*"
A child whispers, "What's a mom in Inuktitut?"
Ina: "Yes! What's a mom in Inuktitut?"
"*Anaana!*"
Ina: "How about a boy, like you?"
"*Irnniq.*"
Ina: "How about a girl, like Kelly?"
"*Panik!*"
Ina: "*Ajungi!*" (Doing good.)

Elaine tells me, "I don't speak Inuktitut, but I'm feeling very soothed that it's around me, because it's a sadness in my heart that I don't speak it. It's around everywhere. Especially in the Ottawa area, no one speaks enough of their own language, so there's a sadness over that. So when I hear it here I know it's one big strong community. And know the children are feeling very comfortable with it."

Ina and Elaine work to provide children with Inuit cultural traditions that are historical, as well as cultural practices that reflect the contemporary life of Inuit people, both in the North and in the city. One morning a student teacher introduces the children to a new material for sensory play—"gak," a gooey mixture of white glue, warm water, and Borax. Out of curiosity, I ask Elaine and Ina if there is an Inuktitut word for *gak*. Looking bemused, they turn to each other and playfully begin to suggest Inuktitut terms for things that are similar to gak in texture and consistency.

Analysis of the case

Liz Lightford is a European Canadian from Ottawa. In a conversation about the issues for teachers who want to implement a cultural curriculum, she articulates their concern. "One of our challenges is to replicate culture authentically in every part of the curriculum. How can we ensure that all the components of the program, including curriculum, room arrangement, behavior guidance, and transitions, are not a token acknowledgement of culture, but are real, authentic, and meaningful?"

Inauthentic curriculum can be described as "tourist" curriculum, which "is both patronizing, emphasizing exotic aspects of a culture, and trivializing, not dealing with the real-life daily problems and experiences of people, but with surface aspects of their celebrations and modes of entertainment" (Derman-Sparks, 1989). As Ramsey suggests,

By knowing how different traits, interests, and activities are regarded by the community, teachers can specifically support the positive group identification of the children in their class. This information can assist teachers in selecting equipment, tools, displays, clothing, props, and materials that both validate children's reference groups and provide opportunities for demonstrating their particular areas of competence. Knowing the social expectations of the community is also helpful, as this will help teachers to foresee and address potential conflicts between cultural identification and the goals of the program. (1987, pp. 114–115)

Children learn culture by playing it

> The child has a hundred languages, a hundred hands, a hundred thoughts, a hundred ways of thinking, of playing, of speaking. (Malaguzzi, 1997)

Vygotsky's sociocultural theory of learning is that children construct knowledge within a cultural context through social interactions with adults and more knowledgeable peers. The results are the specific skills and learning outcomes that are valued by their culture. This theory also emphasizes the concept that symbols—all the various ways that meaning is represented by human beings, including spoken language—are the tools for conveying meaning and influencing the surrounding environment (Berk & Winsler, 1995).

One symbol system that young children use naturally and comfortably is dramatic play. It is one of the "hundred languages" available to children. The play of three-, four-, and five-year-olds, however, has a specific function. Master play is representational. It pictures and reenacts the experiences children have had and can imagine having in the real world, within the safety of the small world of play that the child has created (Erikson, 1950). In play, young children are constructing their knowledge of the world by representing what they know. Play is children's self-chosen process of recreating experience in order to understand it (Reynolds & Jones, 1997).

Vygotsky says that imaginary play is the child's growing edge—in play the child is "stretched" to behave a head taller than himself. Imaginative play is the most effective context for stimulating a young child's cognitive development, because he or she uses symbols to communicate meaning to other skilled players (Berk & Winsler, 1995). In play, the child recreates experience by using symbols that reflect the cultural milieu. Play is socially constructed and dynamic, and children's signifiers may not be understood by other children or may conflict with each other.

Both children who share a common culture and children who have different cultural experiences must negotiate meanings to move their play forward. Skilled players must work out signifiers seamlessly within the frame of their play. For example, two children may not agree whether it is the role of the mom or the dad to cook the fish. To achieve a shared understanding, children need to reinvent and co-construct new ways of signifying and new knowledge. In Piaget's words (1973), "to understand is to invent." For Vygotsky and Piaget, the important cognitive processes developed in play are the invention and internalization of symbols and meanings (Meier & Murrell, 1996).

"Let's play here," says the eager Christian, taking my hand. As an infrequent visitor to the Tungasuvvingat Inuit Head Start Program, I'm glad that a child is inviting me to join his play. I enjoy relating to a child in such a fascinating setting and taking on the role of his partner in play (Jones & Reynolds, 1992) is easy for me. I'm also curious to see if Christian will generate symbols in his dramatic play to express his new knowledge of the Inuits' northern lifestyle. The following are my observation notes, recorded soon after playing with him:

> I quickly discover that my companion is a capable pretend player. In the short time we play together Christian switches roles easily—he is a daddy, mommy, baby, and fish, and he encourages me to play multiple roles as well. Christian's play reveals knowledge of traditional Inuit lifestyle and, with the encouragement of his teacher, he uses some Inuktitut vocabulary. As a city dweller, I assume fireworks are an urban experience, and I ask Christian about seeing them from "out here on the ice" to point out what seems incongruous to me. I wonder if he is describing northern lights, and I am hoping he will expand on the fireworks idea, so I will have some clues as to his meaning. But Christian has a new idea, and I don't want my own questions to interrupt his play.

Later I ask Ina about the children's knowledge of the northern lights. "Not too long ago we were talking about the northern lights," she tells me. "Some of them call them northern lights, but some of them call them fireworks. Some of them have seen northern lights before, but not very many of them. They call them fireworks. They almost look like fireworks, because they go ti, tu, ta. They call it ti, tu, ta."

"What is ti, tu, ta?" I ask.

Pointing to three Inuktitut syllabics on the wall in the children's circle, Ina explains. "That's like these letters here—ti, tu, ta. When they're up in the sky, they look like ti, tu, ta. They go up like this." With her fingers in the air, Ina draws a wavelike motion.

Ina has helped me understand that the children sometimes call the northern lights "fireworks." They also know them as "ti, tu, ta," because these three syllabics are shaped like half-circles that face in different directions. When you put them together as "ti, tu, ta," they form a wave that resembles the wavelike motion of the northern lights.

As Meier and Murrell (1996) caution, well-meaning researchers (and teachers) who don't share the same cultural background as a child need to guard against ascribing meaning to the symbols that the child generates in dramatic play:

> The second issue we want to raise here has to do with how play in culturally diverse communities is construed by observers who are not members of those communities. The fact is that there are many communities in which children do not share the same sensitivities, meanings, and values as the researchers who write in universalistic terms about "children's play." We are advocating a more systematic and careful examination of the social and cultural contexts of children's play. (pp. 101–102)

A head start in bicultural development

In our discussions, college students commonly question the value of racially segregated programs for young children. One student writes,

> Even today at this school (the college environment) you notice how "like" people form friendships; could this be because an opportunity was missed at a very early age to teach children that we are all great and we are all friends? It seems like boundaries are difficult to cross, and it really shouldn't be an issue. I think segregation would just reinforce these feelings of subtle racism. (personal communication, 1998)

To give my perspective on this issue, I describe an early conversation I had with Ina, in which I commented that some of the children didn't "look Inuit." Ina replied,

> Some of the children don't look Inuit! We have four blond Inuit children. They have one white parent. They're Inuit and white mixed—but they all know they're Inuit. They are proud of themselves. We have one child who

came to school and didn't want to be called Inuk because she had brown hair, blue eyes, and looked like white. And she didn't want to be called Inuk at all when we first started. But not even two months she started to ask more about Inuit. "How did they do this? How did we do that?" At the end of the program, when she graduated, she was so proud of herself, who she is; that's a very, very, big thing for us to see, especially myself as an Inuit teacher. Who was not happy being Inuk, look at her now. She is so proud of herself that she's Inuk, she was telling her friends that she graduated from Inuit school. It's a big thing. (personal communication, 1997)

Ina's story conveys this child's pride and her strong sense of Inuit identity. The children have an exceptional opportunity here to develop a sense of themselves as special, different, and uniquely Inuit. An integrated program, even one with a healthy multicultural emphasis, couldn't have this kind of influence on aboriginal children's understanding of their own history, culture, and mother language.

A segregated program can enhance the effectiveness of a child's enculturation process and provide balance in the midst of a contemporary urban way of life. Parents often drop by the program, use the resource center, and sometimes stay to eat. Through these informal opportunities for mutual support, parents help one another learn to maneuver with confidence in the mainstream bureaucratic systems. In this place, with its growing sense of community, both children and parents can practice using their own voices to meet their needs and make their interests known.

Urban areas present special challenges for the survival of aboriginal cultures. These challenges come in part because many of the traditional sources of aboriginal culture—contact with the land, elders, aboriginal languages, and spiritual ceremonies—are difficult to maintain in cities at present. Moreover, aboriginal people are continuously exposed to perceptions, either consciously or unconsciously held, that cities are not where aboriginal cultures belong and can flourish. (Peters, 1996, p. 321)

The value of a segregated program for young Inuit children and their families is affirmed by the argument that the first task in classrooms with children of color is to build their sense of personal and group identity (Derman-Sparks et al., 1989). Phillips emphasizes that the transformation to self-identity cannot be assumed by outsiders. People of color "work toward reclaiming and affirming their racial group identity, and therefore themselves, where the new identity is based on their group's definition of themselves, not the dominant group's definition" (Phillips, 1998, p. 58).

A second task of cultural education is to foster children's bicultural, bicognitive development (Derman-Sparks, 1989), and (where relevant) their biracial identity. Toward this end, a strong grounding in their heritage can complement a child's ongoing, daily acculturation process in the dominant society. Theories of cultural democracy suggest that acculturation into the mainstream, with its emphasis on assimilation and conformity, has negative, subtractive effects on the identity of people of color, "Which—by implication—reduces all other cultural forms to one of inferior value, status, and importance" (Darder, 1991, p. 60). The work of Paulo Freire (1978) suggests that a history of treating people of color as subordinate results in the "habit of submission," an attitude of mind that limits their full ability for critical thinking. The antidote for what Freire calls "socially conditioned dependency" is "critical engagement" in democratic institutions (Darder, 1991, p. 65)—and one of those institutions is school.

Several years of immersion in their culture ensures that Inuit children will have a head start in bicultural, bilingual, and biracial development. I believe that a play-based curriculum supports that goal, because good play empowers young children. In play, young children practice critical thinking skills. They take the initiative, are self-directed, encounter problems, negotiate and resolve conflicts, take one another's perspective, and represent and construct knowledge for themselves.

At play, both children and adults are challenged to invent new solutions to problems within flexible rules and rapidly changing scripts. Playing together, they practice negotiating their varied worldviews to create mutually satisfactory and increasingly complex understandings of their lives. In so doing, children master skills and dispositions that they will need throughout their lives (Jones & Reynolds, 1995, p. 45).

Education for bicultural development also needs to empower the child to take action in the face of racism. Learning to be antiracist takes time, and it isn't too early to begin this work with young children (Derman-Sparks, 1989). How should the teacher respond if she were to overhear, in play, one child say to another, "You can't play with me because your skin is dark"? An important step in the development of children's critical consciousness about racism is to see that their teachers are comfortable talking about it with the children, their parents, and their peers.

> Because racism is ongoing and the subtle messages justifying white privilege are reinforced daily, the work to overcome the influence of these messages on attitudes and behaviors must also be ongoing. It is not possi-

ble to be neutral in this process; you are either part of the problem or part of the solution. As long as the forces to reinforce racist relations in society continue to operate, the individual contributes to their perpetuation unless she actively works to eliminate them. (Phillips, 1998, p. 57)

Discussion questions

My students' responses to this case are often mixed and contain surprises. For students whose experiences in cultural studies are limited, the traditional practices of Inuit people may have an exotic appeal. They ask for curriculum books with prescribed activities that glamorize the culture and don't reflect the people's everyday lifestyles. Other students, planning to teach in environments where the majority of children are of European extraction, may wonder if this case is a waste of their time. Many students question the propriety of segregated programs for any particular cultural group. Also, the question of learning through play always comes up. To encourage students to reflect on the complexity of the issues raised by this case, I pose questions from the following list to stimulate thinking and discussion:

- ▶ Why do you think Inuit families in an urban environment prefer a segregated Head Start program for their children? Do you agree or disagree with their choice, and why?

- ▶ Describe your racial and cultural background to a person near you. Then discuss, as an educator, what you might need to know to teach a program that includes aboriginal children. How can you find out what you need to know? How can you ensure that a curriculum is authentic and reflects the everyday lives of the aboriginal people?

- ▶ How do you feel about working with children whose cultural, social, economic, and language background may be different from your own? How will you approach working with cultural diversity? What will you need to know? How will you find out what you need to know?

- ▶ Do teachers in integrated primary classrooms have special responsibilities to aboriginal and other culturally diverse children?

- ▶ Do you agree or disagree with the concept of play as an appropriate context for construction of knowledge? How can educators who believe in play as an appropriate medium for children's learning communicate that value in diverse cultural contexts?

- ▶ What are the issues that may arise when practices that are appropriate in a particular cultural context don't match recommendations for developmentally appropriate practices?

- ▶ Are you bicultural/bilingual, or do you know someone who is? Should children learn bicultural competence?
- ▶ Do aboriginal children experience racism? Is a preschool program a place where aboriginal children can learn to confront racism? What kinds of skills should these children learn? How can young children be taught these skills?

Section 3

▶▶▶▶▶▶▶▶▶▶▶▶▶▶▶▶▶▶▶▶▶▶▶▶▶▶

Special Needs and Settings

Chapter 9

Helping Parents Take the Lead
Preparing Children for Health Care Procedures

Marcia Hartley, Wheelock College

Introduction

When children are about to experience a painful or anxiety-producing medical procedure, both the children and their families need significant developmental and emotional support. As discussed by Kingson et al. (1996) in chapter 11 of *Playing for Keeps*, in hospitals and medical clinics this role is typically performed by *child life specialists*. These are members of the interdisciplinary health care team whose primary role is to work with children and their families to help them cope with the stresses of illness, treatment, and hospitalization.

In some hospitals and clinics, the health care staff do not accept or encourage the policy of allowing parents to be the main source of their children's emotional support during medical procedures. The most common reason for excluding parents from this process is the fear that a parent in a fragile emotional state may cause the child to become upset during the medical procedure. However, in many cultures parents are accustomed to providing support to their children, especially in highly stressful situations (Loranger, 1992).

The following case describes a four-year-old child who is scheduled for a surgical procedure in a hospital that encourages the parents to be present, and to prepare and support the child throughout the process. It shows one way that both child and parent can be prepared to successfully manage the child's surgical experience.

Jamie and Martha Carlson

Four-year-old Jamie Carlson has been admitted to a hospital's day surgery unit for a surgical procedure. Because of recurrent middle ear infections, *otitis media*, Jamie has been experiencing fever and pain and has missed several school days during the past year. If his ear infections continue, there is the possibility that he might develop a hearing loss. Today Jamie is feeling better, and he has been scheduled for a *myringotomy*—a surgical procedure that involves the insertion of a tiny tube into the tympanic membrane (ear drum) of each ear. This procedure will allow fluid drainage that will relieve the pressure in his middle ears and lessen the likelihood of future infections. For the procedure, Jamie will be given general anesthesia, and he will be ready to return home by the end of the day.

When Jamie and his mother, Martha, arrive at the hospital, they're directed to the playroom for the day surgery unit. This room is a friendly environment where children and parents can play and interact with other families and meet the child life specialist who will prepare them for their hospital visit.

At first, Jamie is hesitant to enter the room and pulls his mother back toward the door. Martha is anxious as well; she's concerned about the general anesthesia that Jamie will be given. Kristen, the child life specialist on duty, rises quickly to greet them and put them at ease. She asks Jamie what he likes to play with at home, and he replies shyly that he likes Legos best. Kristen removes a large box of Lego building blocks from a nearby shelf and places it on a table.

Jamie remains silent. He's hungry and thirsty; to prepare for the anesthesia he's had nothing to eat or drink since the night before. Kristen sits down and begins to build with the Lego building blocks, and soon Jamie and his mother join her and start to create their own buildings. As Jamie's structure takes shape, Kristen comments, "That looks as if it's going to be a very tall building."

"It's a hospital," Jamie replies. He reaches for two small Lego figures—a woman and boy. The child life specialist holds a Lego doctor figure near Jamie's figures and asks, "Why are you coming to the hospital?"

"Earaches," Jamie responds firmly, speaking as the Lego boy figure, "I have to get my ears fixed today."

Using the Lego doctor and family figures, Kristen describes some of the events that Jamie and his mother will encounter this morning. Together the three of them rehearse each stressful situation, giving Jamie a choice of coping strategies. Kristen listens intently to Jamie's questions and concerns, allowing him to lead the conversation; she chooses her words carefully, taking his developmental level into consideration.

When Kristen sees that Jamie and his mother are more comfortable, she brings out a child's medical kit that holds all the medical instruments that Jamie may encounter during his visit. She says, "Mrs. Carlson, could you help me show Jamie what's in this medical kit?" Jamie's mother holds the kit so that he can investigate the instruments, and Jamie pulls out a stethoscope, like those he has seen at his doctor's office. He places the stethoscope on his chest and smiles broadly when he hears his heart beat.

As Martha and Jamie explore the contents of the medical kit, Kristen can see on Martha's face the stress of Jamie's medical procedure. To help relieve her anxiety, Kristen starts to show Jamie and his mother some of the instruments they may encounter that morning. First she shows Martha a pulse oximeter—a small object, about the size of a finger puppet. She explains that it will be placed on Jamie's finger before the procedure, and that it will allow the anesthesiologist to track his heartbeat and the oxygen level in his blood. Martha tries the pulse oximeter on her own finger, and tells Jamie that it feels like a tight-fitting thimble. She is relieved when Jamie tries the pulse oximeter on his own fingers and doesn't seem to mind it.

Next, Kristen shows Martha the kind of face mask that Jamie will have while receiving anesthesia. She describes what Jamie is likely to see, hear, feel, and smell that morning. Jamie has many questions about the anesthesia. Kristen assures him that his mother will be with him in the operating room until he falls asleep. Both Martha and Jamie are very relieved to hear this.

Kristen asks Martha if this is the first time that Jamie has had a hospital experience. Martha tells her that he had surgery when he was two years old, and that she wasn't allowed into either the operating room or the recovery room. For weeks after they returned home, Jamie wouldn't let her out of his sight and wasn't able to sleep alone.

As Kristen continues to describe what Jamie and his mother can expect that morning, Jamie calmly and intently explores the medical kit, trying out the various medical instruments on a teddy bear. Each time Kristen explains something, she's careful to ask follow-up questions to make sure that Martha and Jamie have understood her. She sits with Martha and Jamie until they seem reassured and have no more questions about Jamie's procedure. After their talk, Jamie and his mother continue to play with the Lego building blocks as they await their turn in the operating room.

Later, Kristen accompanies Jamie and his mother to the holding area of the operating room, where she has another box of intriguing toys, designed to help children cope as they wait for their surgery. She stays with them until it's time for Jamie to go into the operating room and accompanies them there.

Jamie's mother stays with him in the operating room until he's fully under anesthesia, and then she returns to the waiting area. Although Jamie's hospital experience has been very stressful for her, she's comforted by the fact that she has been able to stay with him and support him through it.

Analysis

Play is an integral part of childhood. It begins in the early weeks after birth, when parents use soft toys to interest their infants and interact with them. As the parents learn to hold the infant in a soothing way and regulate their facial expressions, voices, and movements to match the child's, a partnership begins that helps the child and parents develop a deep attachment (Bowlby, 1988). Since play is a natural way for parents to interact with a child, encouraging parents to play with a child in a stressful health care setting helps promote normal development.

James Robertson was the first to document on film the severe distress of British children who were receiving medical care in the hospital and not allowed to receive care and emotional support from their parents (Robertson, 1952). In those days, the visiting hours for parents were extremely limited, since the hospital staff feared that visitors might introduce infection. The staff also felt that the parents' visits were undesirable because the children cried each time their parents left.

Today, parental visiting hours are often generous, but parents still face hospital policies that prevent them from supporting their children during a medical procedure. Many hospital staff fear that a parent may become upset and, in turn, upset the child. It seems easier to simply keep parents out of the treatment and operating rooms than to spend the time needed to prepare them to appropriately support their children.

Two views of the child life specialist's role

Currently, there are two models for the child life specialist's role in providing support services for children receiving health care. As described by Kingson et al. (1996, p. 143–149) in chapter 11 of *Playing for Keeps*, these two opposing points of view can be summarized as a play-based focus and a restructured role with emphasis on medically oriented interventions, such as preparation for, or support during, a procedure.

Play-based focus: The first model is a play-based program, in which the child life staff maintains a family-friendly environment for the children and their parents. This room is designed to be the setting for play and informal discussions. The activities include both directive and nondirective play that allows children to learn about their health care experiences, express their feelings about them, and identify ways to cope with their experiences. By observing and interacting with the children and their parents during play, the child life staff can learn about the needs, anxieties, and learning styles of the children and their families. The playroom also allows both parents and children to interact with and gain support from their peers.

The drawback of this model is that although the play opportunities are plentiful, the responsibility of managing the playroom activities may prevent the child life staff from preparing all the children for their procedures. Also, the staff lacks the flexibility to accompany children and parents during anxiety-producing procedures in order to coach the parents at that critical time.

Restructured child life role: The second model uses dolls and medical instruments primarily as a teaching tool, to assess, teach children and parents, and provide support. Here, the management of the playroom activities is delegated to assistants who provide "general developmental and diversional play." The child life specialist concentrates on focused interactions or interventions, such as systematically preparing children for procedures, rehearsing coping techniques, and supporting the child during the procedure.

The drawback of this model is that, although a parent may be present in the treatment room, it is primarily the child life specialist who provides comfort and support to the child during the procedure. In this model, the role of the parent as the child's primary, trusted advocate seems to be of secondary importance. Also, as a child prepares for surgery, using play as a tool to facilitate development has a lower priority than preparing the child for the procedure.

A third way

The case of Jamie and Martha shows a third model, in which a child life specialist seeks to involve a parent fully in preparing her child for the medical procedure. The child life specialist uses play to facilitate developmentally appropriate learning and coping strategies, so that the parent can remain with her child and provide support until the child goes under anesthesia.

In this proposed third model, the child life specialist provides the parents with information about the procedure and encourages them to use developmentally appropriate language and props to teach and support the child. With the parent in control, the child life specialist has the flexibility to support other families. One advantage of this approach is that the child life specialist is able to serve more families.

As Shelton and Stepanek (1994) advise, the caregivers who are a child's primary source of emotional and developmental support at home should be allowed to retain their accustomed role of chief advocate during the health care experience. In the case described above, the child life specialist encouraged Martha in this role by fully informing her about his procedure. This reduced her anxiety and empowered her to comfort her son.

By helping children and parents learn new concepts and develop positive ways of coping with difficult circumstances, the child life specialist facilitates family-centered care. The American Academy of Pediatrics (1993) recommends that adequate play facilities under the direction of child life specialists be provided in all pediatric settings. Child life programs are available in many hospital units, including pediatrics, intensive care, outpatient clinics, and emergency departments, as well as in home care and day programs for children with long-term conditions.

Regardless of where the child life services are rendered, it's important to document the child life specialist's observations and services in the child's medical record. This provides a useful tool for communicating with the other members of the health care team and for training students. The psychosocial services that support the child's development and emotional well-being should be documented in the medical record. The child life specialist's observations of the child and family interactions in the relatively normal environment of the playroom can often give the interdisciplinary team valuable insights into the child's development and the family's needs.

Discussion questions

▸ What would be a primary developmental need for most five-year-olds receiving health care?

▸ How would you respond to a parent who is hesitant to provide emotional support to a child during a procedure? What information and support could you offer to enable the parent to remain with the child and provide emotional support?

▸ In order to discover any possible misconceptions, the child must actively participate in the preparation process. How could you use puppets or play to encourage a child to interact with you?

▸ As the child life specialist, how would you document a case in a child's medical record so that the interdisciplinary staff reading it would learn more about the child's development and the use of play?

▸ How is the use of play in a hospital setting different from play in other settings?

Suggested readings and resources

Bolig, R. (1986). Unstructured play in hospital settings: An internal locus of control rationale. *Children's Health Care, 15* (2), 101–107.

Bolig, R. (Ed.). (1988). Play in health care settings [Theme issue]. *Children's Health Care, 16* (3).

Bolig, R. (1990). Play in health care settings: A challenge for the 1990s. *Children's Health Care, 19* (4), 229–233.

Bolig, R. (1991). Medical play and preparation: Questions and answers. *Children's Health Care, 20* (4), 225–229.

Gaynard, L., Wolfer, J., Goldberger, J., Thompson, R., Redburn, L., & Laidley, L. (1990). *Psychosocial care of children in hospitals: A clinical practice manual from the Association for the Care of Children's Health Child Life Research Project.* Bethesda, MD: Association for the Care of Children's Health.

Robertson, J. (1970). *Young children in hospital* (2nd ed.). London: Tavistock.

Chapter 10

Roundabout We Go
A Playable Moment with a Child with Autism

Amy Phillips, Wheelock College

Introduction

This case centers around ten minutes that I fondly remember from my early professional life as an art teacher and play therapist in a school for children with autism. It describes my first encounter with six-year-old Teddy. I happened to be in a position to assist while Teddy's teacher had her hands full with several other students. I hardly knew the youngster, but I did know that he was so absorbed that I'd have to start with his preoccupations if we were to take a productive path—and I believe that we did end up playing together.

In chapter 8 of *Playing for Keeps*, Meier and Murrell (1996) plead eloquently for educators to honor the varied manifestations of play in our culture. Any dominant culture will tend to "standardize" the way that individuals organize their behavior, to use anthropologist Gregory Bateson's term. The play of children with autism doesn't have a standard appearance and is not "preferred in the culture" (to use another of Bateson's terms), and can thus tend to isolate them from full entry (Meier & Murrell, 1996).

In chapter 10 in *Playing for Keeps*, Marchant and Brown (1996) recommend that special educators look to play as a source for context-rich interactions with all children. They also encourage regular educators to consider how to shape play with children with special needs to make it available to them for learning. My play with Teddy arose from years of experience with children with autism, during which I had found play to be the golden road to constructive engagement—and sometimes the only way to build a relationship. With children who would otherwise engage only minimally, I often felt closest when we had puppets on our hands or toy cars on the table between us. Had Teddy and I not played, I'm certain that we would have had more difficulty getting to know one another as we later did.

Teddy in the Library

I hear a tumbling sound emanating from the open doorway to the school library. Peering in, I see six-year-old Teddy busily dumping books on the floor. With a raised eyebrow I consult his teacher—who is busy reading a story to the other children—and get her nonverbal assent to get involved.

Before taking action, I watch for a moment. Teddy is turning in a full circle, repetitively scooping up books from the shelf and dumping them on the floor. Energy buzzes from every taut muscle; I can almost see it spiraling off him as he twirls. I take stock. I realize that I barely know this little whirlwind. I can see that he is full of a purpose of his own. I can see that he is pretty good at whirling and dumping. I know that he rarely talks, and then only with words that he seems to be echoing from the ends of other people's sentences. I've heard that his tantrums can be sudden and violent. I decide on one thing, at least. We don't know one another well enough for me to try anything as radical as confronting this implacable antilibrarian head-on.

I consider my alternatives. It seems clear that Teddy is unlikely to be interested in stopping what he is doing or becoming involved in anything else. He's paying absolutely no attention to me. Every ounce of his attention is on his actions. And yet I don't know what those actions mean to him, if anything. Did he just get stuck in this repetitive loop, as sometimes seems to happen with children with autism? Is he mad about something and taking it out on the books? Is he playing "library" in his own unique way? Is he enjoying the chance to take things that are all lined up and dump them all together? I don't know. I decide to assume the best and figure that he's having fun. However, if this is a game of some kind, I'm not part of it at all.

With the benign perversity so necessary in this kind of work, I decide to try to join in Teddy's play. But what can I do? There seems to be little room for me in his spiral of energy. Children with autism often repeat the same actions over and over again, and these repeated actions can be very hard to deflect. This preference for routine, repetitive actions—called self-stimulation (often abbreviated as "stimming")—is one of autism's primary characteristics.

Then I remember something that I'd seen on a visit to another school for children with autism. The instructors in that school would deflect the characteristic repetitive gestures of stimming through a sort of martial arts pirouette, which was effective in diverting the children from their flapping or rhythmic leaping; they would settle down and sit quietly in a chair or stand in line. By joining their energy with the energy of the child's movements, the instructors were able to redirect it.

This memory gives me an idea, and I look around for a way to shift Teddy's movement stream. My eyes settle on a broad-seated metal chair; which I pick up and place next to Teddy. In doing so, I project an air of service and anticipation, as in pulling out a chair to help someone take his seat.

As I had hoped, Teddy begins piling the books onto the more reachable chair surface, rather than the floor. This is indeed a much faster way to dump books. I help by tidying the books on the chair seat, thus making room for more. Although Teddy still hasn't acknowledged my presence, he has accepted my contribution to his activity. This is a start, I think—at least he hasn't barred me from playing my own game. I announce with pleasure, to no one in particular, "See how the library books were all on their shelves, and then Teddy made them all pile about the floor, and then Amy found a chair. And now Teddy piles them all up on its seat and now Amy is helping him make bigger, neater piles!"

For a while we play our two "games"—Teddy creates the piles and I straighten them. However, soon the chair fills up, and Teddy seems reluctant to use the floor again. I say loudly to myself, "Library books go *out* and come *in*," as if discovering something of great delight. I start to reshelve the dumped books at the empty end of the shelf, while Teddy continues to remove them from the other end. I check to see if this reshelving perturbs Teddy, but he seems unconcerned by my innovation. He appears more concerned with the process of removal than with the production of an empty shelf. We continue in this way for some time, unstacking and restacking the shelf with what have now become "our" books.

Teddy's teacher notices that our activity is a bit unusual, and she starts to speak firmly to Teddy. Taking the chance that she'll forgive me when I explain later, I say loudly. "We're discovering that library books get checked *out* and then they get returned and come *in*. I'm playing the restacker and maybe Teddy is playing the 'taker-outer.'"

Teddy seems to accept what I'm up to. Our pace increases, and I talk out loud about the new roles I've assigned to us. "My restacking job is becoming much easier. Books are ready on the chair just as I need them to be." I begin to feel that we are in this together, playing a new game—that we are sharing a few moments of mutual enterprise. I decide to up the ante. I gesture to Teddy to de-shelve the next section of books. Together we remove and restack the entire next section, then we move to the next shelf—and Teddy waits until I have repositioned "our" chair and myself. He looks at the perfectly placed chair, looks right at me for the first time, and grins. I grin back. In no time we have neatly removed all the books from this shelf and put them back again. I feel pride in our work—and Teddy's precise movements and smiling face tell me that he does, too. Our relationship has begun.

Analysis

Teddy's behavior posed a puzzle, and I knew that I had to solve this puzzle *with* him. What did his activity mean to him? What was he up to? What was he getting out of it? How might he react to my intervention? What could I do that he might tolerate or even appreciate? What could we do together? I would have to act based on whatever I knew. I could simply try to stop him—but I knew that I'd have more success if I tried to see things from Teddy's point of view and get him to see things a bit more from mine.

If I had known Teddy better, I would have had a great asset in deciding what to do. I could have built on my understanding of his strengths, his loves, his preoccupations, his amusements. I might have known whether he was inclined to act like this whenever there were things to take off shelves, if he was acting out a library game, or if there was something that was setting him off at this particular time.

I could see that Teddy was very absorbed in de-shelving the books. I decided to build on his obvious strengths: energy, intensity, and tolerance of my (nonintrusive) presence. Later, I wanted to build on the sense of fun that I could feel growing between us. As we "played" together, it seemed that we began to share a perspective, even an agenda. This was encouraging, because I sensed that it was only through sharing that I would be able to make a difference to the problem at hand.

The scenario that I was witnessing was right at the heart of the challenges that children with autism both pose and experience. According to the fourth edition of the *Diagnostic and Statistical Manual of Mental Disorders* (American Psychiatric Association, 1994), children with autism have these deficits: "markedly abnormal or impaired development in social interaction and communication and a markedly restricted repertoire of activities and interests" (p. 66). I could see all of these elements in Teddy's absorption, his lack of response to my presence, his wordlessness, and his whirling repetitive action without attention to the teacher's story or the contents of the books he was dumping. I knew that I would have to respect the challenges that Teddy was posing as well as his strengths.

I couldn't rely on normal verbal communication, such as questions and answers. At six, Teddy's language skills were still quite delayed. That is why I chose to communicate through actions instead. I knew that Teddy would respond to me more readily if I were a moving entity rather than a thinking and talking entity. The language that I did use was very simple, and it paralleled our actions. The words reinforced what Teddy was seeing, hearing, and doing. Saying "Library books go *out* and come *in*" was a way of completing a circle of movement. While I didn't expect Teddy to suddenly grasp the meaning of "library," this might engender some idea of "in and out," or at least putting books back in might become as interesting as taking them out had been.

In addition to the communication challenge, I also knew that Teddy and I didn't have a common understanding of one another as social beings. In fact, to Teddy any direct attempt at engagement might feel like an unwarranted and indecipherable intrusion. However, since his behavior was likely to feel intrusive to others, he needed to realize that he shared a world with others, to learn to tolerate and even welcome other people into his world.

For Teddy to accept me as a force in his world, I would need my actions to be congruent with his and with others already in his world and become a useful and interesting force to him. My actions would need to be as close to his as possible. I chose noninvasive extensions—slight reshapings of his energy flow. My actions did not require Teddy to read my social cues, but they did offer him a tempting pathway that was more connected and constructive than his own. As our connection grew stronger, my reshaping grew more determinative—I went from helping Teddy dump the books to presuming that he would tolerate my reshelving them.

I took my cues from what I could see: a boy repeatedly dumping books on the floor. Teddy's fierce concentration on his "interest of the moment" told me where to start, so that I could kindle an interaction. Donna Williams, describing how to build interactions with people with autism (such as herself), also recommends beginning with the child's perspective and avoiding head-on confrontations:

> This method, in complete contradiction to normal interaction, is indirect in nature. In this way it is less all-consuming, suffocating, and invasive. The child can then reach out, not as a conforming, role-playing robot, but as a feeling, albeit extremely shy and evasive, human being. The best approach would be one that would not exchange individuality and freedom for the parents', teachers', or counselors' version of respectability and impressiveness. (1992, p. 201)

We have learned from people with autism that what appears to be mindless repetitive behavior can be a richly felt experience with intense inner meaning. It can be so compelling, we are told, that it's difficult to avoid getting lost in the richness of the experience and also difficult to share it with other people. They say that nonautistic people can help if we do not simply squelch these patterns of behavior, but instead build on them (Williams, 1992, 1996; Grandin, 1995). In this case I tried to do this by helping Teddy extend his play from a solitary, enveloping act to an interdependent dance.

Was Teddy really "playing"?

It's entirely possible that Teddy was playing some sort of game, although he couldn't explain what it was. One of the prime diagnostic descriptors of children with autism is that they become locked into routines—and a routine can become a passionate necessity. People with autism report that there are often other things going on when they appear to others to be behaving in aimless, obstructive, or destructive ways.

For example, during free art time one youngster appeared to be randomly lining up his markers. Through gentle conversation, I discovered that he was playing a precise and long-running game, with rules that demanded an intricate orchestration of color composition. His willingness to fill me in on the intricate details of his game seemed to show that he appreciated the chance to share his interests. In turn, I introduced him to other artists, and we were both pleased when his game evolved in response.

I found another youngster with autism lying across the school hallway at a right angle to the flow of traffic, with his feet touching one wall and his hands the other. Nothing worked to dislodge him until I asked him if this was a funny joke, at which point he leapt up and went guffawing down the hall.

Intervention with children with autism is most effective when it is based on the meaning that the children are making for themselves. We must choose our guidance wisely, since it will help determine the child's social understandings. Meier and Murrell caution us not to impose our own meanings on children's play because "the child's plane of consciousness is formed in the structures that are transmitted to the child by . . . others in speech, social interactions, and interactions of cooperative activity" (1996, p. 109). Although I clearly had a standard of library use, within that standard Teddy would have to enjoy the library in his own way, whether it was to explore the physical depths of the bookshelves, the concepts of order versus chaos, or the ideas contained in the books.

Conclusion

When we work with children we must often ask, "What should I do about this?" and make our choices fast. As we make those choices, we must monitor what happens and choose among the options that unfold. In order to respond with certainty and sensitivity, we must call upon our accumulated skills and wisdom and the relationships we have built with the children. With children who are trying to make sense of a confusing world, as Teddy was, we are often confronted with an almost impenetrable puzzle about what to do. This tests our skills, our wisdom, and our capacity to make connections and respond sensitively. If we aren't successful, we may contribute to the child's confusion, making the child feel even less connected and competent than before. Every encounter can help a child make more sense of the world, gain more control over her own behavior, and feel more connected to others.

Discussion questions

Questions for group discussion

One approach to discussing this case is to begin by asking students to consider how they would react if they came upon Teddy dumping library books in their own milieu. This might initiate an open-ended discussion covering the following topics:

- What would your own perspective on this situation be? What alternatives would you see? What play elements would you be able to share with a child whom you don't know very well? How else might you interact in a playful manner? Would you act as Amy did?

- Could you act as Amy did? How compartmentalized are your roles and responsibilities? Is your setting a place where you would feel welcomed or discouraged from using a playful approach? Would you feel pressure to stop the child immediately, or could you take some time to observe the situation and play with it a bit?

- Based on this case, are there any lessons to be learned for your own practice and setting? Would you make any suggestions about practices in your own setting? With what other sorts of children and incidents might an approach like this one be helpful?

Questions for written or small-group assignments

Another approach to discussing this case is to assign questions such as the following to individuals or small groups as preparation for discussion:

- What do you think was going on from Amy's perspective?
- What do you think was going on from Teddy's perspective?
- Why is it important to understand play from the player's perspective?
- In your opinion, was Teddy really playing?
- What led Amy to believe that Teddy was playing, or to pretend to believe it?
- How might you handle this sort of incident in the setting in which you work with children?
- How else could an adult have handled this scenario in a playful manner?

Chapter 11

Eddie Goes to School
Facilitating Play with a Child with Special Needs

Betty Noldon Allen, Tufts University and
Cheryl Render Brown, Wheelock College

Introduction

This is a case study of Eddie, a five-year-old boy who has a diagnosis of cerebral palsy. This case is most relevant to chapter 10 in *Playing for Keeps: Supporting Children's Play* (Marchant & Brown, 1996) because it exemplifies the principle that the role of play in young children's development must be carefully planned and used to facilitate children's learning.

The analysis of this case is based on the idea that there is a continuum of adult involvement in children's play, depending upon the needs of the individual child. Marchant and Brown refer to this as a continuum from nondirected play to guided play to directed play (p. 132). It's important to note that this idea runs counter to the more romantic belief that adults should not involve themselves at all in children's play. When supporting children who have difficulty initiating or sustaining play with their peers, we have often heard fellow teachers say, "You can't make kids play with someone they haven't chosen." However, in this case, all the members of Eddie's teaching team subscribed to this approach and used Eddie's therapeutic sessions to facilitate his interactions with other children.

The case focuses on Eddie's first year in a university-affiliated laboratory school. At the time of his entry, Eddie was not a verbal communicator, which made it difficult for him to initiate and sustain playful interactions with his peers. Four- and five-year-old children are typically at the stage of highly imaginative and collaborative play, which relies heavily on hearing and language.

One point that Eddie's case illustrates is that when a child lacks verbal ability, it can be difficult to make an accurate assessment of his or her potential. When Eddie entered the laboratory school, he had just begun to use Mayer-Johnson communication pictures. These are picture cards that allow nonverbal communicators to make requests or converse with others by pointing to pictures that are arranged by topic. For example, to indicate activity choices, the cards depict balls, wagons, and swings in the playground, and blocks, art, and modeling-clay tables in the classroom. One question that faced Eddie's team at his entry was how the Mayer-Johnson pictures might facilitate his play with other children.

Eddie's background

At the time described in this case, Eddie was five years old and living with his mother, father, and three-year-old sister in suburban Boston. He had been diagnosed with cerebral palsy at birth, after an uneventful pregnancy. The right side of Eddie's body was most affected by his disability, especially his right leg. When walking, he would drag his right foot a bit, and his right arm would sometimes hang at his side. In general, Eddie could get around well, although he had some difficulty with balance and lifting his right foot and tended to stumble over obstacles.

The weakness of Eddie's right arm was quite limiting, and he required prompting to use the arm (for example, when carrying his lunchbox). Ordinary classroom activities, such as holding writing utensils, removing caps from markers, and holding a piece of paper in place, were very challenging for him.

Despite his physical limitations, Eddie's primary way of interacting was to move about, especially outdoors. Although he was highly social, he was not a verbal communicator. At the time of this case (age five), he could say a few words—"Mama," "hi," "bye," "peepee," "daddy," and "Nicky" (his sister's name). He also knew some sign language ("all done" and "more") and he could nod and shake his head for "yes" and "no."

The laboratory school

As a toddler, Eddie had entered a half-day special needs classroom in his public school, which he attended for two years. When he was five years old, his parents requested a transfer to a different school, where he could have a full-day program and be mainstreamed with typical peers. In response to this request, the public school referred his parents to a university-affiliated laboratory school in the greater Boston area. This school, which focuses on children from infancy to age six, provides research and training for professions that involve working with children, such as teaching and psychology.

The laboratory school appointed a team to evaluate Eddie's admission and plan his program (a typical team might include a resource teacher, a speech therapist, and a program director, as well as other professional staff). The resource teacher observed Eddie in his public school classroom and gathered information to share with the laboratory school team to help determine Eddie's eligibility and needs. Once the team had determined that their program was appropriate for Eddie, their next task was to plan a full-day program for him. They decided that because of his special needs, Eddie would fit best into their multiage group of three-to-five-year-olds who had various levels of functioning and a range of play behaviors.

The plan that the team developed for Eddie divided his school day between two groups. In the morning he would attend a multiage group that would provide the bulk of his cognitive stimulation. In the afternoon he would attend a program with a smaller group of multiage children that would focus on social interaction skills. In the morning, Eddie would have the support of both Jamila, his teacher, and Denise, a one-on-one paraprofessional who was a graduate teaching assistant with an interest in inclusive teaching practices. In the smaller afternoon group, Eddie would receive help from his teacher, Brooke, and would be encouraged to be more independent.

During the summer before school began, Eddie and his parents visited his new classroom space and met the staff who would be working with him. They reviewed Eddie's full-day plan and phase-in schedule. Jamila, Brooke, and Denise visited Eddie's home to observe him in that setting and get to know him better. Eddie's physical therapist from the public school (who would still be working with him at his new school) visited the laboratory school to help the staff anticipate potential challenges and plan modifications.

When school began, Eddie's speech therapist gave an in-service training for the staff about using the Mayer-Johnson cards and other nonverbal communication tools, such as topic boards and communication books.

The staff arranged monthly progress meetings with Eddie's family and the public school liaison to follow Eddie's progress (a step that isn't necessary for a child who is developing typically). The staff created a home/school communication log, which Jamila, Brooke, Denise, and Eddie's therapists used to keep his parents informed. In addition, Denise had a weekly phone date with Eddie's family.

Eddie's play-based curriculum

The peer-picture concentration game

Jamila and Brooke realized that one way that they could help Eddie improve his play skills would be to help him develop the ability to identify his classmates by name. Eddie's classroom included an attendance board with removable pictures of all the children. Using the pictures on the board, they created a concentration game, in which Eddie and one of his peers would take turns turning over a picture, finding that child in the classroom, and then returning for another turn. This was an adaptation of the Mayer-Johnson communication system that Eddie was already familiar with.

The tower of blocks

At first Eddie loved to knock down the towers of blocks that his peers had carefully built up. Jamila and Brooke wanted to encourage him to build with blocks himself; they also wanted to include more give-and-take with his peers to increase his play capacity. To address these two goals, Eddie's physical therapist created a two-person game for him to play during his scooter-board therapy time on the wheelchair ramp in the hallway. First Eddie and his play partner would build a tower of large cardboard blocks. Then Eddie would ride down the ramp on the scooter board to knock them down, while his partner called out, "One, two three, go! . . . Okay, now it's my turn." At that point, the two of them would build up the tower of blocks again. Eddie and his peers loved this game, and it also addressed the therapist's physical goals for Eddie, including posture and balance.

Rest and meeting times

In the beginning of the school year, rest time was very difficult for Eddie—he wasn't able to stay on his mat for five minutes. In response, his teachers developed a plan that Eddie would rest for a few minutes, and then walk around the school. These walks included negotiating stairs and exploring sound-making materials (a giant xylophone and other musical instruments) to give Eddie some physical therapy and bring him pleasure, since he loved music.

The morning meeting time, which could last up to twenty minutes, was another difficult period for Eddie. His teachers decided to deal with this challenge proactively, to ensure that he wouldn't establish the habit of acting up in order to be taken out of the room. They began by having Eddie stay only for the musical part of the meeting. After that, he would leave the group (accompanied by Denise) and work with his speech therapist. As the school year progressed, the amount of time that Eddie spent in the meeting was gradually increased, and eventually he was able to stay for the entire time.

Finding a good seat for Eddie was another struggle. His cube chair was too low and did not give him the proper support. Placing him on a riser meant that he was farther away from the teacher and not directly in front of the storybook at reading time. Without this closeness and focus, it was harder for him to pay attention.

Separation

Separation was another area of difficulty for Eddie. This was unanticipated, although in retrospect it should not have been. At the beginning of the school year, Eddie would become tearful at leaving time and would repeat "Mommy" all day; sometimes he would go to the door and forlornly repeat "Mommy."

Later Eddie went through a period where he would burst into tears at lunchtime. This was difficult for the other children because they wanted to comfort him and were unable to. They would cover their ears when Eddie cried, and the staff became worried that no one would want to sit with him. This was also frustrating for the staff, because Eddie couldn't verbalize why he was crying, and they couldn't comfort him, either. Although they didn't know why Eddie was crying, they assumed that he must be thinking of home. Since this behavior made Eddie a less attractive playmate, they felt that it was critical to address it.

The crying began just after Eddie had been home for a week with a bad cold. As the staff reflected on this, they recalled that in his first days at the school Eddie had found it difficult to eat surrounded by the stimulation of the other children, so he had eaten lunch in the therapy room with the occupational therapist. They returned to this routine, and Eddie was gradually able to work back to eating lunch in the classroom. However, he didn't stop crying until both his teachers and his parents told him that he had to stop it.

The following vignette illustrates a sequence that Denise facilitated to initiate Eddie's social interactions.

The red wagon

Denise pulled Eddie in a red wagon on the playground. It was "outside time," and all of Eddie's classmates were outdoors too. Eddie's red wagon was sitting beside the triangular path that served as a thoroughfare for the children's vehicles. Julie was pedaling a tricycle furiously around the triangle. Ian, who had been watching Eddie and Denise, stood beside the path. Ian picked up a short leafy branch and started using it to direct traffic—lowering it in front of the wagon to signal "stop!" and then raising it to signal "go!"

Denise stooped down and asked Eddie, "Are you ready to *go?*" while signing "go." Eddie looked at her and nodded. Denise said, "Yes," and pulled Eddie's wagon onto the path. Ian jumped forward and lowered the branch in front of the wagon.

Denise knelt down again and asked Ian, "Do you want him to *stop?*" while signing "stop." When Ian replied, "Yes," Denise said to Eddie, "Ian wants you to *stop,*" again signing "stop." "Okay? Remember, Ian, this sign means *stop.*"

While this was going on, Eddie sat in the wagon and calmly watched the activity around him. Then he signed "more" to indicate that he wants Denise to resume pulling the wagon. Denise said, "Okay, we can *go* now," signing "go."

Denise pulled Eddie's wagon around the path several more times, and each time she approached Ian, he said, "Stop," and Denise stopped the wagon. When Ian signaled "go," they resumed their movement. Eventually,

Eddie began to smile at Ian, acknowledging their interaction. After a while another child, Hillary, came over and asked for a turn pulling Eddie along. Denise said to Eddie, "Hillary wants to pull you in the wagon."

In this game, Denise's goal of encouraging Eddie's peers to interact with him met with initial success. Their later play sequences involved Eddie pulling others in the wagon and alternating turns with others.

Analysis

Eddie's games at school extended his attention span, increased his play interactions (first with Denise and later with his peers), and enhanced his ability to communicate by using a total communication system including verbal communication, picture cards, and signing. These abilities allowed Eddie to become a truly functioning member of the classroom.

One of the things that the team learned in using a total communication system with Eddie was that his receptive language exceeded their initial expectations. The system not only enhanced Eddie's expressive language, it also allowed his peers to better understand and appreciate him as a learner, and gave his teaching team a window into the capabilities that were masked by Eddie's lack of verbal expression.

The teaching staff also introduced Eddie's peers to these new modes of communication so that they could initiate play with Eddie. For example, at snack time all the children could use the food pictures to choose their snacks. Also, the playground activity picture cards were placed on a loose-leaf ring that children could use to interact with Eddie during outdoor time.

Social Interactions

Much of the staff's work with Eddie involved facilitating his social interactions on the playground and in the classroom. Although he was very social in intent, they had to work on ways to make his peer interactions longer and more meaningful. Some of these ways included

- ▸ arranging play dates with other children in the group
- ▸ making a lotto game out of the children's photographs as a way for Eddie to identify his game partners
- ▸ introducing sign language to the class and explaining why Eddie talked with his hands

- introducing communication boards to the class and using them to select songs at meeting time, explaining Eddie's disability, using the term *cerebral palsy*

Eddie's classmates had many questions, and some of them wanted to take care of him. While this intention was admirable, his teachers used various approaches to help the other children see Eddie's capabilities, as well. They promoted conversation and read books about children and adults with disabilities to explain why it was hard for Eddie to do some things that the other children could do easily, such as toileting and talking fluently.

The other children continued to have questions about Eddie, and the teachers' goal was to maintain an atmosphere in which they would feel comfortable asking those questions. For example, they initiated a curriculum project in which each child introduced herself to the group by completing a page about herself. On his page, Eddie "wrote" that he had cerebral palsy and a different way of communicating.

Another focus was continuous work on Eddie's self-help skills, especially toileting. He made progress, although slowly. As Eddie improved, the staff was able to decrease the frequency of the meetings with his parents that they had arranged at the beginning of the school year.

Discussion Questions

- What strengths does Eddie have that his teachers could build upon? What are some ways that they might begin that process?
- How could a teacher discuss Eddie's challenges with his peers, while encouraging them to see him as a competent individual?
- What should Eddie's teacher expect from him as a learner in this kind of classroom setting?
- How might Eddie's teachers promote and encourage more social interactions? (Consider his inappropriate social behavior, which included prolonged crying and also grabbing other children and holding them too tightly.)
- During Eddie's periods of inconsolable crying, what might the staff do to support (a) Eddie; (b) the other children; and (c) one another?
- How might play with other children be further used in Eddie's therapy (speech, physical, occupational) to scaffold his social interactions?

▸ What additional assessments (such as the use of communication or technology tools) might give Eddie's team more information and lead to better educational planning for him?

▸ What role might technology play in facilitating Eddie's social interactions in this setting?

Suggested readings and resources

Dormans, J. P., & Pellegrino, L. (1998). *Caring for children with cerebral palsy: A team approach*. Baltimore, MD: Brookes.

Smith, T., Polloway, E. A., Patton, J. R., & Dowdy, C. A. (1998). *Teaching students with special needs in inclusive settings* (2nd ed.). Needham, MA: Allyn & Bacon.

Wolery, M., Strain, P., & Bailey, D. B. Jr. (1992). Reaching potentials of young children with special needs. In S. Bredekamp & T. Rosegrant (Eds.), *Reaching potentials: Appropriate curriculum and assessment for young children: Vol. I* (pp. 92–111). Washington, DC: National Association for the Education of Young Children.

Chapter 12

"Every Time They Get Started, We Interrupt Them"
Children with Special Needs at Play

Frances Henderson, Pacific Oaks College (former), and
Elizabeth Jones, Pacific Oaks College

Introduction

"Tell me about the play of the children you know," Elizabeth (Betty) Jones asked the students in her Pacific Oaks College class, Play in Childhood. The students went around the circle, talking in turn. When Irma's turn came, she explained, "I teach a special education class for developmentally delayed children. Our children don't play."

"Really?" Betty asked. "I would have thought that all children play."

"I'll go back and watch," Irma said.

The next week Irma reported her findings to the class. "They do try to play," she said. "But every time they get started, we interrupt them."

I (Fran) am also a special education teacher who took Betty's class. This chapter describes what I've been learning about supporting the play of three- to five-year-old children who have special needs in my classroom. Because the Play in Childhood class took place online, Betty and I have a complete record of our dialogue about these experiences, some of which is included in this chapter. It reveals how we learned from one another in the process.

I will describe four scenes in which I set the stage for children's play, and then observed their engagement with their play materials and each other. The children have amazed me, their parents, and my colleagues, with their growth in initiative and ability to communicate. I love watching these children make sense of their world. I'm ever amazed at their determination, their hunger for knowledge, and—most of all—the fun they seem to be having. Children with disabilities have the same right to fun and friendship as other children; it's up to us to provide them with opportunities to pursue these experiences.

Marchant and Brown (1996) emphasize the importance of encouraging play in all children, while discussing some of the practical and theoretical reasons why play may not be emphasized in inclusive programs. Because many physical and developmental disabilities lead to slower response times, children with special needs may need extra time to create and sustain play. Often, however, they get less time than other children. They are likely to be scheduled for testing, therapy, and interferences of various kinds during their participation in the usual preschool day.

Because individual educational plans and concern for the children's safety may promote dependence, children with special needs typically have reduced opportunities for taking the initiative, taking risks, and making choices. However, choosing and inventing play is the most important cognitive challenge that young children face. Children whose play initiative is restricted will become less competent than their potential (however limited) would allow.

The following observations all took place in my class of three- to five-year-olds at a nonprofit agency in Hemet, California (a small community about one hundred miles east of Los Angeles). Our agency offers in-home and classroom programs and child care to all the children with special needs in the community, from birth to age seven. The children whose stories I tell here have been diagnosed with a variety of special needs, such as Down's syndrome, autism, cerebral palsy, global delays, and communication disorders. Many have multiple handicaps.

My class, which averages about fifteen children, typically has a staff of six or seven, for a three-to-one student-teacher ratio, as well as aides who shadow some children one-on-one. Our three-hour morning program also shares outdoor space and activities with the two- to four-year-olds in the class for typically developing children.

Scaffolding Play

Hannah and Donald are sitting in the block area, each playing with the contents of a box of toys. Donald's box contains large wooden blocks; Hannah's contains people and furniture from the dollhouse. Donald is stacking his blocks; Hannah is picking up the toy people, who are scattered about the carpet. She licks the doll she is holding, and then puts it in the box.

Donald sees Maggie, the speech therapist, enter the room. He runs over to her and slaps her hands in a high five. When he leaves, Eduardo comes over and sits down next to the box of blocks. He begins to throw them across the rug. Hannah imitates him, throwing blocks toward the same area.

I've been observing their play from across the room; now I approach them and say, "Let's build." I put down a block, and Eduardo places a block on top of it. Hannah returns to picking up dollhouse furniture. Maggie joins us and sits down. "Look, put on top," she says, stacking blocks. "Let's make a house." Eduardo says, "House." He pushes over Maggie's stack. "Down."

Maggie stacks the blocks again. Hannah puts a block on the stack. "Put on top," says Maggie. The blocks fall over. "Uh-oh," says Maggie.

Hannah begins to dig through the box of people. Then she looks up at Maggie and Eduardo's new stack and knocks it down. Eduardo laughs: "Down."

"Hannah, put on top," Maggie says, demonstrating. Hannah turns back to her box and throws some of the toys out. She picks them up and puts them back again. Eduardo knocks over Maggie's stack again: "Down." Hannah knocks over the remaining blocks: "Yea." She claps her hands, stacks three blocks, knocks them down, and claps again. Maggie hands her another block, and Hannah repeats the stack, knock down, clap sequence several times; so does Eduardo.

Maggie says, "Do more." She stacks more blocks, then picks up two and hits them together. Holding them over her head, she says, "Do up high." Hannah imitates her: "Down! . . . Yea." She claps, picks up some blocks, and puts them in her box, then picks up two more and hits them together.

Maggie builds a road with blocks and drives a car down the road. "Push the car," she says. Eduardo and Hannah both imitate her: "Push! . . . Down!" Hannah breaks up the road, then she turns to Fran, says "Hi," and climbs onto her lap for a hug.

Analysis

As we have learned to scaffold children's movement to the next level of play, the children play more. The more we support children as they play, the better they play. I have shared pictures of some of our children's block buildings with their parents, who were delighted and amazed by the structures their children had built. Several expressed a desire to buy wooden blocks for building at home. My boss was so amazed that she offered to buy me a larger set (which I had been asking for). I think the program gave away its block sets years ago because the children were hitting each other with them.

For example, the children have become aware of changes in their play. Donald built a wonderful block tower yesterday. I took a picture of it and taped it to the wall in the block area. I showed him the picture this morning, and he stood in front of the picture, touching the tower, and then sat on the floor gazing at it as he went back to work. He built a tower that was completely different from the one he made yesterday, and he kept looking back and forth between the picture and the blocks as he built.

Teacher commentary

Fran: Hannah has been wandering less since she went on antibiotics to clear up a chronic sinus infection, but as you can see, her play has not developed much beyond putting in, taking out, and imitation.

Betty: Well, if she were fifteen months old instead of four years, we would see putting in, taking out, and imitation as just what she should be doing. When assessing the play of developmentally delayed children, it's helpful to think in terms of the developmental sequence. Also, her knocking down blocks became more than simple imitation of Eduardo—for both of them it became a reciprocal game, a motivation for stacking. You build so you can knock down, as any toddler knows: "Down!" "Yea!" Knocking down is a more dramatic variant of putting in and taking out, and it makes your friend laugh. If your teacher is paying attention, she'll laugh too.

Fran: What sticks out in bold print for me so far are your words, "Mastery of physical skills and language is a precursor of master play" (Reynolds & Jones, 1997, p. 7). The children in our class do not have mastery over physical skills and language characteristic of their chronological age, and so their functional play is limited.

Betty: Yes! I believe that learning to play is crucial for developing intelligence. So if your children need help with physical mastery and with language, you provide all the help you can. But the goal is to be able to play—to initiate, to accomplish for oneself. This is the developmental task in the preschool years.

Play as an Educational Goal

Margarita came to our program at age four-and-a-half from a Head Start program whose staff had decided they couldn't help her—she would spend the morning either crying or galloping around the room with a string or ribbon flying behind her. She is the middle child and only daughter of Spanish-speaking parents. She was diagnosed at age three with autism spectrum disorder and at four with mild to moderate hearing loss, for which she wears hearing aids; she may also be mildly mentally retarded, although that has been difficult to test.

When she entered our program in September her hearing aids were broken and I wasn't aware that she normally wore them. She was very fretful, crying and engaging in much self-stimulation ("stimming")—picking up strings and ribbons, running in circles around the room, sitting in a sandbox or at a tactile bin pouring sand through her fingers. It was not until early November that she wore her hearing aids to school, and then she was very quiet—sitting in empty corners and not attempting to play. She made no sounds and communicated only by leading an adult to what she wanted (usually food).

In late November we finally got a Spanish-speaking aide, Alma. Alma shadowed Margarita, looking for ways to involve her in classroom activities and walking her through them. She worked with her for about an hour a day outside the room, beginning with compliance and imitation (the first step in communication) and using a combination of Spanish, sign language, and PECS (picture exchange communication system). Then Alma began to generalize what they were working on during classroom time, and as she did so, Margarita slowly began to participate in the play centers and to actually appear to enjoy what she was doing. We often paired her with Eduardo, a Spanish-speaking child with Down's syndrome, who has an uncanny sense of other children's needs.

Within a year, Margarita was transformed. She now makes eye contact, spontaneously greets us with a smile or a hug, and uses PECS to communicate her requests. She is able to generalize what she has been taught and spontaneously use it in a new play situation later. She will participate in parallel play with another child and is beginning to use sequence play. This week she brought play food over to a couple of the teachers for them to sample. Yesterday she put on dress-up clothes, looked at herself in the mirror, smelled the artificial roses she was wearing, and glided around the room. Today she marched in from the bus, hung up her backpack, picked up a baby doll, gave her a kiss on the nose, and sat rocking her in a chair, feeding her with a bottle. She has also begun to involve herself in the daily tasks that lead to independence such as dressing, toileting, serving herself lunch, carrying her backpack, and walking off the bus (her mother had been carrying her). What a change from last year, when she just sat on a mattress all day!

Teacher commentary

To me, this is a phenomenal change. Margarita is unable to speak, and it's really hard for many children with autism to communicate with people. Nevertheless, she now attempts to communicate with people who don't even speak the same language her family does. I think that shows a real desire on her part to join our world and not remain isolated in the private world that she had been living in.

Alma goes to Margarita's home one day a week and works with Margarita, her little brother, and their mother, to show them things that they can do with Margarita at home. Margarita's family was as amazed watching her dress a doll as they were watching her dress herself; they did not know that she was able to do these things. Margarita's mother told us the other day that she had only bought Margarita things like ribbons, because she thought that was the only play Margarita was able to do and she wanted her to have something to do for fun. When she first saw Margarita feed a baby doll at home, she cried.

> Play is the child's natural way of learning; it provides the time and opportunities children need to construct their own knowledge. . . . Mastering play is as important as mastering oral and written language. All these modes of symbolic representation enable human beings to remember, to manage, to plan, and to communicate with each other. (Reynolds & Jones, 1997, p. 1)

Fran: I often write play goals for children's IEPs. The speech therapists love play goals, because they know that's where speech is apt to occur! It is quite possible to write a goal for more complexity in a child's play: "The child will become a more complex player" (Reynolds & Jones, 1997; Jones & Reynolds, 1992).

I have learned over the years that it is next to impossible to insist that a child participate in an activity that doesn't interest the child. Even the most disabled child will simply close his or her eyes and disappear! ("I can't see you—you can't see me.") However, goals such as the following can all be met in play:

- ▸ "Child will play alongside another child."
- ▸ "Child will interact with another child in a play situation."
- ▸ "Child will improve play skills."
- ▸ "Child will use sign, verbalizations, or computerized voice with a peer or adult."
- ▸ "Child will achieve (specific occupational or physical therapy goals)."

Betty: As you're saying, the most significant aspect of play is that it's self-motivated. Play is what you or I or any child *want* to do. To get children to stop playing so we can make them do something else is the age-old challenge that adults face in their dealings with children. It's much more efficient to try for a win/win solution—"Where is the intersection between what you want to do and what I want you to do?" And that not only saves adult energy, it also allows the child the power of choice, building self-esteem and a sense of competence—which are surely major challenges for any child who has special needs. The issue, I think, is whether the teacher is able to shift the center from her agenda to the child's, to support the child's disposition toward autonomy and initiative (power *with*) rather than insist on attention to her goals (power *for/on*) (Jones & Reynolds, 1992).

Fran: We do get children who engage in very little spontaneous play. When we first knew Margarita, she alternated between stimming and just sitting. To build a relationship with her and challenge her to grow, Alma stayed with her, guided her physically into activities, and worked with her on tasks that weren't chosen by Margarita, using food rewards. In introducing her to the picture communication system (PECS), Alma would offer her snack choices: "Do you want juice or milk? Fish crackers or wheat thins?"

Betty: Why is it necessary to push a child to communicate?

Fran: Typically, developing children communicate without being pushed, although most parents are quick with spontaneous positive reinforcement. Margarita, with her autism and hearing impairment, doesn't speak, and her signing is minimal. The PECS picture cards give her the ability to participate, and not always just be pushed or carried through life. (Until recently, her mother carried her to the bus, although she was perfectly capable of walking.) Margarita had to learn to communicate her basic wants before she could move on to social play and more complex communication. We keep looking for adaptive communication supports for Margarita, just as we did with Alix (whom we provided first with a walker and then with a talker). Margarita has begun to use the computer and enjoys it immensely. She draws scribbles—a form of constructive play-and she enjoys games such as *First Words* (in Spanish), which help build receptive communication skills. Over time, the computer may become a significant choice for her communication.

Betty: So the issue for some of your children is getting them started, and the direct approach to that is positive reinforcement of their primitive motives (such as food) to gain compliance with an adult's requests. The indirect approach would be to observe the child in minute detail, looking for clues to the child's motivation to explore and for opportunities to reinforce play and build on bits of spontaneous action. That's where scaffolding comes in. You have described several of your children, including Hannah, as "wanderers"—and have wondered, thoughtful teacher that you are, if you were missing some small attempts at play. Wandering might be a form of stimming, rather like the pacing of caged tigers, but it could also be how the child checks out the territory. I think your challenge is not simply to interrupt wandering, but to look very carefully for a "hook" for a play intervention. Your observation of Hannah with the blocks was a fine example of an adult joining in, responding, offering new materials and play possibilities.

Emergent Curriculum

Airplanes

Recently we have noticed that the children have been drawn toward the toy airplanes, so we made a team decision to try a rather loose lesson plan around this new interest. From around the school we gathered up books, records, big planes, little planes, paper planes, people, Lego building block airports with all their goodies, airplane puzzles—whatever looked interesting and developmentally appropriate for our classroom. The results included the following delightful moments:

- Evan came to find me to show me that the propellers on the top of the helicopter and those on the front of the airplane were the same.

- Brent (who has autism and needs help with social skills) met his goal for reciprocal turn-taking by flying planes with a classmate.

- Everyone joined in the fun of flying paper airplanes across the room and cheering them on.

- We showed a video, *There Goes an Airplane* (filmed at the local airport). Afterward several children indicated that they wanted to see it again. They also used their toy aircraft to imitate the sounds and flight patterns they had seen in the film.

- Outdoors, we pointed out the planes and helicopters flying overhead (and had many pointed out to us).

- We joined in as several children moved chairs across the room to make a plane and signed for us to sit down in the seats.

- Even the children who weren't ready for propellers or videos danced enthusiastically to Hap Palmer's "My Hands Are High" and "Going on a Trip."

We were surprised at the number of children who looked intently through the books about planes, wheels, and flying that we had added to the bookcase, and asked us to read them again and again. We all (adults and children) learned a lot.

Dinosaurs

Now we're doing the dinosaur thing. It never ceases to amaze me how much preschoolers (and other children) love dinosaurs. We will continue with this as long as it holds the children's interest. Sam and Lenny put together a seven-piece interlocking dinosaur puzzle today, roaring like tyrannosaurs all the while. I have never before seen either of them complete even a four-piece puzzle, although puzzles are available every day. They worked together to figure out where all the pieces fit. After minimal scaffolding on my part, they were fingering the pieces, looking for the curvy part that fit here, or the feet that belonged on the ground.

Almost all the children have learned the sign for "dinosaur," and we just can't keep them away from the toy dinosaurs. Three children made clay dinosaurs, another first. This was the first time that any of the children have made a representation of anything in a medium other than paint or crayon—not that we haven't tried!

Teacher commentary

Betty: My observation of special education programs suggests a clear distinction between traditional behaviorist approaches and scaffolding for play. Behaviorists set imposed goals in the IEP—that is, the goals come from the adult, not the child. Although they are derived from observing the child, this is diagnostic observation, looking for the child's skills, not the child's interests. It's a deficit model—"How can we fix this child?"— in which the teacher insists that the child engage in goal-oriented activities. (The deficit model is imposed on children in most educational systems; as a lively third-grader who had formerly been in a progressive school sadly said of her new classroom, "They find out what you can't do and make you do it and do it.") Constructivist approaches, on the other hand, begin by trying to identify the child's motivation: "What is this child interested in? What play scripts are potentially inherent in those interests?"

Spontaneous play is the behavior through which healthy children learn. A child who has handicaps will have to be supported in moving toward increasingly complex play. In a group of children a curriculum will emerge that builds on shared interests while supporting skill development.

Your dinosaurs are a good example. You provided dinosaur puzzles as part of the general environment, but you didn't plan a dinosaur curriculum; that came from the kids. Is it the ferocity and size of dinosaurs that make them so enchanting to kids, who are basically fierce but frustratingly small? Sam and Lenny's new-found puzzle-making competence is a lovely example of the zone of proximal development—children increase notably in competence when they're doing something they're excited about and get only helpful hints from an adult. Vygotsky called that "scaffolding"—adult input that enables the child to do more, on a self-selected activity, than she could do alone (Berk, 1994).

Fran: I think you may be right. They love the fact that they can roar and it's acceptable because they're dinosaurs. For days we've been roaring to the bathroom, to the therapy room, and all around the yard!

Betty: Did you experience anxiety when we first started discussing the concept of letting curriculum emerge, rather than doing detailed lesson plans for each week?

Fran: My first reaction to this concept was that my children weren't verbal enough to make much headway toward an emergent curriculum. However, we're beginning to allow the children opportunities to guide us more in developing classroom activities.

Betty: Your reaction surprises me! If you taught toddlers or young two-year-olds, would you assume that you couldn't make much headway toward emergent curriculum because they "aren't very verbal"?

Fran: No, I sure wouldn't. But when we discussed emergent curriculum in your class, the other students' stories all contained so much child language. It was hard to see how it could happen in our classroom. Now I see it working, but on a different level!

Betty: The teachers of children who are further along developmentally can really get into the representation of experience—language, dramatic play, and all the arts. Younger children, children who are in the sensori-motor stage, aren't representing their experience—they're just doing it. A child who has just discovered how to stand upright doesn't need to say anything about it; it's enough to be standing there.

Fran: Yes, yes, that is our class. We simply do it! I feel better about this now. We spend much more time on basic developmental tasks than in a typical classroom, but the tasks *are* being mastered. The crawlers are walking, the walkers are running, the children are self-feeding, pedaling their bikes, making friends, stacking blocks, learning sign language.

Although I miss the wonderful verbal communication of other three- and four-year-olds, we are certainly communicating ideas gesturally and through sign. Several of the children are waiting for communication systems that will give them a "voice" and open up their world. And now that we have given Alix and Nicki ways to be upright, they have begun playing house.

Betty: Children stand up and walk before they begin dramatic play— of course! So what adults need to do is to provide the assistance that makes spontaneous developmental behavior possible?

Fran: Yes, and it will happen. Our staff has talked at length about motivation this year. Some children are more motivated than others, and some need intervention to get going, but everyone shows excitement about

143

something. We draw on many of the "sources of emergent curriculum" (Jones & Nimmo, 1994). "Living together"—conflict resolution, self-help skills—these are big topics in our room. This group has much interest in "people in their environment"—bus drivers, secretaries, counselors, teachers, big kids, housekeepers. They want to know them all, and luckily for us, most of them are willing to share their time and their laps in our room.

Which brings us to "serendipity." In our classroom, we have learned to go with the flow. The unexpected happens quite often, and we decided long ago that it was far better to incorporate the unexpected than to ignore it. Some of our favorite days have been those kinds of days!

Adding Complexity in the Sandbox

Yesterday I added a Little Tykes table, two funnels, four see-through measuring cups, and two small pitchers to our sandbox, which is usually equipped only with buckets, shovels, and trucks. The response was amazing—the other teachers came up to congratulate me on my brilliance! The children flocked to the sandbox to stand up at the little table and play. There was much imaginative play and conversation, not only from my children, but also from the two- and three-year-olds in the yard. Adding the table changed the sandbox play from simple scooping and dumping activities into play kitchens, with cakes baking and pitchers of drinks being offered. It was great fun.

Today was another wonderful day. We had water play outside for most of the morning. Eduardo joyfully cleaned all of our chairs and the doll furniture. He was so careful, flipping things over to make sure that he cleaned both sides! He had many helpers. The teachers next door, noticing our fun, threw caution to the wind (everyone had a change of clothing) and let their kids join in. We all had a terrific time, and there were lots of choices to be made. Some of the children played with bubbles and wands, some washed babies, some played in the sprinklers or with squirt bottles, and some did everything.

Teacher commentary

Betty: From this description, I would never know that these are "children with special needs." They're simply young children, competently and joyfully at play. The children's spectacular response to the new materials in the sandbox reminds me of a research finding that some child care programs for two-year-olds showed a tendency to "dumb down" the environment because the children were young:

> Yards that served younger children were decidedly less interesting than those designed for three- and four-year-olds. . . . While two-year-olds probably need a simpler environment than older children, we have the feeling that many yards for two-year-olds may well elicit and maintain what is commonly called typical two-year-old behavior. For instance, we observed a yard . . . in which the most important problem for children was finding something interesting to do next. Because they were two-and-a-half to three, "next" would come quite often; and because of the minimum complexity "next" would most likely be a shift from unit to unit, rather than a broadening of interest and involvement within a single complex unit. In other words, the yard offered little opportunity to increase attention span." (Kritchevsky & Prescott, 1969, pp. 26–27)

Does it seem to you, Fran, that this may also happen in settings for children with special needs? And that one reason adults have to help children focus on activities is that there isn't enough in the physical environment to compel children's interest?

Fran: Yes, I think that happens a lot. Staff are often reluctant to provide "too much" because it will all have to be cleaned up, and it will soon be time for toileting, anyway. I find that I am introducing far more "loose parts" than I used to—playfully, really, to see what will happen—and I'm always fascinated by the outcomes. With more of this sort of stimulation, the children become more competent than I would ever have expected.

I brought back some sand from the beach and put it out in tubs today. It was amazing what an attraction it was, even though we have a large sandbox in the yard. Beach sand, because it is so soft, is a completely different experience. The kids stayed with it all morning. The shells, seaweed, and magnifying glasses were also big hits!

Alix spent a great deal of time on the "beach," complete with beach towels, a radio, a picnic set with fried chicken and watermelon (made of plastic), baby dolls, sunhats, and books about the beach. She has just gotten a small personal "talker" and loved asking people to come to the beach or play babies with her.

Betty: The beach experience sounds very exciting. I keep seeing that developmentally delayed children become more competent when they have opportunities for more complex and awe-inspiring activities like this.

I wonder how much their developmental delay gets aggravated by segregating them and not including them in the activities that other children are likely to experience?

Fran: Other teachers are beginning to stop by our room and comment or ask questions, which is a good sign. My boss has asked me to do an in-service this summer on play and the teacher's role. She likes what she's seeing and hopes that it will be picked up by some of those more resistant to change. I promised to include "loose parts." It's funny how those kids will play with dishes and pots and pans if you put them in the sandbox!

Conclusion

Fran: Thanks so much for focusing my mind on play this year. It is wonderful to have a sounding board for some of the thoughts I've carried around with me for a long time. Such good things keep happening. The differences we have seen in many of our children over the last couple of months have been simply amazing. They're doing so much better in my class that I am very interested to see how they will do out in the regular school world.

Discussion questions

- ▶ Why is it that so many adults think that children with special needs do not know how to play? How can we help to counter this notion?

- ▶ What helped the author realize the power of play for her students with special needs?

- ▶ How can talking about children's play lead teachers such as this one to a deeper understanding of their children?

- ▶ Was Fran and Betty's correspondence an effective form of professional development? Why? Do you think it would work for you?

References

Acker. E. (1923). *400 Games for school, home, and playground.* Danville, NY: F. A. Owen.

American Academy of Pediatrics Committee on Hospital Care. (1993). Child life programs. *Pediatrics, 91,* 671–673.

American Psychiatric Association. (1994). *Diagnostic and statistical manual of mental disorders* (4th ed.). Washington, DC: Author.

Bartolini, V. (1996). On-the-job training: Children's play and work. In A. L. Phillips (Vol. Ed.), *Topics in early childhood education: Vol. 2. Playing for keeps: Supporting children's play* (pp. 119–126). St. Paul: Redleaf Press.

Beaty, J. (1996). *Skills for preschool teachers.* Englewood Cliffs, NJ: Prentice Hall.

Berk, L. E. (1994). Vygotsky's theory: The importance of make-believe play. *Young Children, 50* (1), 30–39.

Berk, L., & Winsler, A. (1995). *Scaffolding children's learning: Vygotsky and early childhood education.* Washington, DC: National Association for the Education of Young Children.

Bernhard, J. K., Lefebvre, M. L., Chud, G., & Lange, R. (1997). The preparation of early childhood educators in three Canadian areas of immigrant influx: Diversity issues. *Canadian Children, 2,* 26–34.

Billig, M. (1997). Keeping the white queen in play. In M. Fine, L. Weis, L. Powell, & L. M. Want (Eds.), *Off white* (pp. 149–157). New York: Routledge.

Billman, J. (1992). The Native American curriculum: Attempting alternatives to tepees and headbands. *Young Children, 47* (6), 22–25.

Bowlby, J. (1988). *A secure base: Parent-child attachment and healthy human development.* London: Routledge.

Bredekamp, S., & Copple, C. (Eds.). (1997). *Developmentally appropriate practice in early childhood programs.* Washington, DC: National Association for the Education of Young Children.

Carlsson-Paige, N., & Levin, D. (1998). *Before push comes to shove: Building conflict resolution skills with young children.* St. Paul: Redleaf Press.

Carter, M., & Curtis, D. (1994). *Training teachers: A harvest of theory and practice.* St. Paul: Redleaf Press.

Cooper, R. M. (1996). The role of play in the acculturation process. In A. L. Phillips (Vol. Ed.), *Topics in early childhood education: Vol. 2. Playing for keeps: Supporting children's play* (pp. 89–98). St. Paul: Redleaf Press.

Cornelius, C. (1998). *Iroquois corn in a culture-based curriculum: A framework for respectfully teaching about cultures.* New York: State University of New York Press.

References

Cortés, C. E. (2000). *The children are watching: How the media teach about diversity.* New York: Teachers College Press.

Darder, A. (1991). *Culture and power in the classroom: Critical foundations for bicultural education.* New York: Bergin & Garvey.

De Gaetano, Y., Williams, L. R., & Volk, D. (1998). *Kaleidoscope: A multicultural approach for the primary school classroom.* NJ: Merrill.

Derman-Sparks, L. (1993). Empowering children to create a caring culture in a world of differences. *Childhood Education, 2,* 66–71.

Derman-Sparks, L., & ABC Task Force. (1989). *Anti-bias curriculum.* Washington, DC: National Association for the Education of Young Children.

Dowd, F. S. (1992). Evaluating children's books portraying Native American and Asian cultures. *Childhood Education, 68* (4), 219–224.

Else, P., & Sturrock, G. (1999). The playground as therapeutic space: Playwork as healing. In M. Guddemi, T. Jambor, & A. Skrupakelis (Eds.), *Play in a changing society* (pp. 20–25). Little Rock, AR: Southern Early Childhood Association.

Erikson, E. H. (1950). *Childhood and society.* New York: Norton.

Freire, P. (1978). *Education for critical consciousness.* New York: Seabury Press.

Fung, H. (1994). *The socialization of shame in young Chinese children.* Unpublished doctoral dissertation, University of Chicago.

Goleman, D. (1995). *Emotional intelligence.* New York: Bantam Books.

GossMan, H. (1992). Meeting the needs of all children—An Indian perspective. In B. Neugebauer (Ed.), *Alike and different: Exploring our humanity with young children.* Washington, DC: National Association for the Education of Young Children.

Gragg, C. L. (1940). *Because Wisdom Can't Be Told.* Boston: Harvard Business School, Case # 451-005.

Grandin, T. (1995). *Thinking in pictures: And other reports from my life with autism.* New York: Doubleday.

Greenberg, P. (1992). Teaching about Native Americans? Or teaching about people, including Native Americans? *Young Children, 47* (6), 27–30, 79–82.

Hall, N. S. (1999). *Creative resources for the anti-bias classroom.* Albany, NY: Delmar.

Hernandez, H. (2001). *Multicultural education: A teacher's guide to linking context, process, and content.* Upper Saddle River, NJ: Prentice Hall.

Hesse, P., & Poklemba, D. (1994). *Rambo meets the Care Bears: Responding to children's television in the classroom.* Cambridge, MA: Center for Psychology and Social Change.

Hudson, S., & Thompson, D. (1999). Reducing "risk" on playgrounds. In M. Guddemi, T. Jambor, & A. Skrupakelis (Eds.), *Play in a changing society* (pp. 61–62). Little Rock, AR: Southern Early Childhood Association.

Hyun, E. (1998). *Making sense of developmentally and culturally appropriate practice (DCAP) in early childhood education*. New York: Peter Lang.

Johannessen, L. (2000, Spring). *Encouraging active learning with case studies*. Paper presented at the meeting of the National Council of Teachers of English, New York.

Jones, E., & Nimmo, J. (1994). *Emergent curriculum*. Washington, DC: National Association for the Education of Young Children.

Jones, E., & Reynolds, G. (1992). *The play's the thing: Teachers' roles in children's play*. New York: Teachers College Press.

Kingson, J. F., Thompson, R. H., Allen, K. E., Boettcher, C., Collins, T., & Goldberger, J. (1996). Implementing play in hospitals: Values and viewpoints. In A. Phillips (Vol. Ed.), *Topics in early childhood education: Vol. 2. Playing for keeps: Supporting children's play* (pp. 141–157). St. Paul: Redleaf Press.

Klein, A. (1996). Constructing knowledge about play: Case method and teacher education. In A. L. Phillips (Vol. Ed.), *Topics in early childhood education: Vol. 2. Playing for keeps: Supporting children's play* (pp. 57–66). St. Paul: Redleaf Press.

Klugman, E. (1995). *Play, policy, and practice*. St. Paul: Redleaf Press.

Klugman, E. (1996). The value of play as perceived by Wheelock College freshmen. In A. L. Phillips (Vol. Ed.), *Topics in early childhood education: Vol. 2. Playing for keeps: Supporting children's play* (pp. 13–32). St. Paul: Redleaf Press.

Kritchevsky, S., & Prescott, E. (1969). *Planning environments for young children: Physical space*. Washington, DC: National Association for the Education of Young Children.

Lakin, M. B. (1996). The meaning of play: Perspectives from Pacific Oaks College. In A. L. Phillips (Vol. Ed.), *Topics in early childhood education: Vol. 2. Playing for keeps: Supporting children's play* (pp. 33–43). St. Paul: Redleaf Press.

Lee, E., Menkart, D., & Okazawa-Rey, M. (Eds.). (1998). *Beyond heros and holidays: A practical guide to K–12 anti-racist, multicultural education and staff development*. Washington, DC: Network of Educators on the Americas.

Levin, D. (1994). *Teaching young children in violent times: Building a peaceable classroom*. Cambridge, MA: Educators for Social Responsibility.

Levin, D. (1996). Endangered play, endangered development: A constructivist view of the role of play in development and learning. In A. L. Phillips (Vol. Ed.), *Topics in early childhood education: Vol. 2. Playing for keeps: Supporting children's play* (pp. 73–88). St. Paul: Redleaf Press.

Levin, D., & Carlsson-Paige, N. (1995). The Mighty Morphin Power Rangers: Teachers voice concern. *Young Children, 50*, 67–72.

Levin, D. E. (1995). Media, culture, and the undermining of play in the United States. In E. Klugman (Ed.) *Play policy and practice*. St. Paul: Redleaf Press.

Levine, R. (1980). A cross-cultural perspective on parenting. In M. D. Fantini and R. Cardenas (Eds.) *Parenting in a multicultural society*. New York: Longman.

References

Lopez, G. (2001). Revisiting white racism in educational research: Critical race theory and the problem of method. *Educational Researcher, 30* (1), 29–33.

Loranger, N. (1992). Play intervention strategies for the Hispanic toddler with separation anxiety. *Pediatric Nursing, 18* (6), 571–575.

Malaguzzi, L. (1997). *I cento linguaggi dei bambini* (The hundred languages of children). Reggio Emilia, Italy: Reggio Children.

Mann, J. (1998, April 1). Looking into the young heart of violence. *The Washington Post,* p. T20.

Marchant, C., & Render Brown, C. (1996). The role of play in inclusive early childhood settings. In A. L. Phillips (Vol. Ed.), *Topics in early childhood education: Vol. 2. Playing for keeps: Supporting children's play* (pp. 127–139). St. Paul: Redleaf Press.

McLane, J. B., Spielberger, J., & Klugman, E. (1996). Play in early childhood development and education: Issues and questions. In A. L. Phillips (Vol. Ed.), *Topics in early childhood education: Vol. 2. Playing for keeps: Supporting children's play* (pp. 5–12). St. Paul: Redleaf Press.

McWilliam, P. J. (1992). The case method of instruction: Teaching application and problem-solving skills to early interventionists. *Journal of Early Intervention, 16,* 360–373.

Meier, T., & Murrell, P. (1996). "They can't even play right!": Cultural myopia in the analysis of play—cultural perspectives on human development. In A. L. Phillips (Vol. Ed.), *Topics in early childhood education: Vol. 2. Playing for keeps: Supporting children's play* (pp. 99–113). St. Paul: Redleaf Press.

Morrow, L. M. (1990). Preparing the classroom environment to promote literacy during play. *Early Childhood Research Quarterly, 5,* 537–554.

Moyles, J. R. (1990). *Just playing? The role and status of play in early childhood education.* Philadelphia: Open University Press.

Oldsen, G., & Rudney, G. (1995). Undergraduate writing case studies: Opportunities for reflection and dealing with dilemmas. *Teaching and Learning, 10* (1), 16–23.

Pellegrini, A. D., & Galda, L. (1993). Ten years after: A reexamination of symbolic play and literacy research. *Reading Research Quarterly, 28,* 163–175.

Peters, E. (1996). Aboriginal people in urban areas. In D. A. Long & O. P. Dickason (Eds.), *Visions of the heart: Canadian aboriginal issues* (pp. 305–333). Toronto: Harcourt Brace, Canada.

Phillips, A. L. (Vol. Ed.). (1996). *Topics in early childhood education: Vol. 2. Playing for keeps: Supporting children's play.* St. Paul: Redleaf Press.

Phillips, C. B. (1998). Preparing teachers to use their voices for change. *Young Children, 53,* 55–60.

Piaget, J. (1973). *To understand is to invent.* New York: Grossman.

Prescott, E., Jones, E., Kritchevsky, S., Milich, C., & Haselhoef, E. (1975). *Assessment of child rearing environments: An ecological approach: Part II. An environmental inventory.* Pasadena, CA: Pacific Oaks College.

Ramsey, P. G. (1987). *Teaching and learning in a diverse world: Multicultural education for young children*. New York: Teachers College Press.

Reynolds, G., & Jones, E. (1997). *Master players: Learning from children at play*. New York: Teachers College Press.

Robertson, J. (1952). *A two-year-old goes to hospital* (video), Ipswich: Concord Films Council. New York: New York University Film Library.

Schrader, C. T. (1990). Symbolic play as a curricular tool for early literacy development. *Early Childhood Research Quarterly, 5*, 79–103.

Seefeldt, C. (1997). *Social studies for the preschool-primary child*. Columbus, OH: Merrill.

Shelton, T., & Stepanek, J. (1994). *Family-centered care for children needing specialized health and developmental services*. Bethesda, MD: Association for the Care of Children's Health.

Slapin, B., & Seale, D. (1992). *Through Indian eyes*. Philadelphia: New Society.

Spielberger, J. (1999). *Head Start teachers' beliefs and representations about the role of pretend play in early childhood development and education*. Unpublished doctoral dissertation, Erikson Institute, Loyola University, Chicago.

Tudge, J., Lee, S., & Putnam, S. (1995). Young children's play in socio-cultural context: Examples from South Korea and North America. Expanded version of a paper presented in *The pretend play of cultures: Cultures of pretend play*. Symposium conducted at the meeting of the Society for Research in Child Development, Indianapolis.

Tungasuvvingat Inuit Head Start Program. (1997). *Parent handbook*. Ottawa: Author.

Viorst, J. (1972). *Alexander and the terrible, horrible, no good, very bad day*. New York: Atheneum.

Vygotsky. L. (1978). The role of play in development. In M. Cole, V. John-Steiner, S. Scribner, & E. Souberman (Eds.), *Mind in society: The development of higher psychological processes*, (pp. 92–104). Cambridge, MA: Harvard University Press.

Wachtel, P. L. (1999). *Race in the mind of America*. New York: Routledge.

Williams, D. (1992). *Nobody nowhere: The extraordinary autobiography of an autistic*. New York: Random House.

Williams, D. (1996). *Autism: An inside-out approach*. London: Jessica Kingsley.

Williams, K. (1994). *An examination of personal storytelling in black middle class families*. Unpublished doctoral dissertation, University of Chicago.

About the editors

Cheryl Render Brown, M.Ed., is an associate professor at Wheelock College. For the last four years she has been the chair of Wheelock's Faculty Play Research and Study Group, which has taken a leading role in the Early Childhood Consortium publications on play. For the last six years she has coordinated Wheelock's graduate early childhood education program. In addition to coediting this volume, she also coauthored a chapter in this volume and a chapter in the second book of this series.

Cheryl leads a monthly forum for faculty who supervise student teachers, interns, and new teachers in public and private child care and education settings. Cheryl's nonacademic projects include consulting with a group of seventeen towns to help them provide inclusive programming for children with special needs and their typical peers. She is also working as the site coordinator for Wheelock in the federally funded Head Start early childhood higher education faculty initiative.

Cheryl lives in Framingham, Massachusetts, with her husband, Leonard. Her most valuable learning about play has been provided by her children, Omrao, Sashi, and Samira, who continue to play vigorously in their adulthood.

 **Catherine Marchant, Ed.D.,** is an early childhood teacher educator who works with prospective and practicing teachers on issues related to young children's learning and development. She is a faculty member at Wheelock College and a coach/consultant with the Boston Plan for Excellence in the Public Schools. In both positions, she aims to connect her understanding of learning and teaching to the realities of classroom life and school practices.

Catherine has written about the developmental processes associated with learning to teach, preschool teachers' perceptions of inclusion, and the impact of in-service training on teachers' beliefs about the social needs of students with AD(H)D. In schools and community settings, she is a strong advocate for the rightful place of play in children's lives and learning, and loves working with children in the Boston public school system.

In addition to coediting this volume, Catherine co-authored a chapter in the second book of this series. She lives in Brookline, Massachusetts, with her husband, Ed, and her children, Eliot and Cameron.

About the chapter authors

Betty Noldon Allen is a lecturer and the coordinator of student teaching for the prekindergarten to grade 3 program in the child development department at Tufts University. A teacher educator, she received a B.A. in early childhood education from Simmons College and an M.Ed. in early childhood special needs from Lesley College. She was a classroom teacher for a number of years, and served as the special needs resource teacher for the Eliot-Pearson Children's School before assuming teaching and administrative duties for the child development department.

Betty conducts workshops on topics such as inclusion, understanding behavior, and anti-bias education for early childhood professionals in the Boston area. She is a member of a faculty group that is in the process of writing a parenting guide. Betty lives in Brookline, Massachusetts.

Jillian Ardley, Ph.D., is the senior coordinator for the Family and Pre-School Program in Morganton, North Carolina. She has a degree in early childhood education from Florida State University and has been an assistant professor at Wheelock College and Clark Atlanta University. Jill has also held teaching positions at the pre-school, elementary, and university levels and has been involved in teacher training, preparation, and supervision in urban areas. She wrote her chapter for this book while she was a faculty member at Wheelock College.

Jill's research emphasis is developmentally and culturally appropriate practices, and she has published teaching tools and publications within this area. She is presently working on training tools for preservice teachers and providers for culturally diverse families who have young children with special needs.

Vicki Bartolini, Ph.D., has taught part-time at Wheelock Graduate School for the last eight years; she is also a full-time faculty member at Wheaton College. Her research focuses on the evaluation of birth-through-five family support programs and the development of mentoring programs to support preservice, beginning, and veteran teachers. She has received numerous competitive grants to support her research and also does consulting on mentoring and program evaluation.

Vicki helped establish a Wheelock off-campus master's program in Attleboro, Massachusetts, where she also helped to develop a community partnership program that was recently honored. Vicki has a manuscript under review on the evaluation of family support programs for ages birth through five. She lives in Franklin, Massachusetts.

Lisa M. Ericson is a kindergarten teacher in Groton, Massachusetts. She received both an M.S. in early childhood education and a B.S. in human development from Wheelock College in 1998.

In her classroom Lisa places great emphasis on the value of play in children's social, emotional, and academic learning. She continues to grow in her understanding of the value of play, with the help of her 23 five-year-old teachers.

Lisa coauthored her chapter in this book with Jill Ardley (her faculty supervisor) while completing her graduate study at Wheelock College. Lisa lives in Lowell, Massachusetts.

Marcia Hartley, M.S., is a faculty member at Wheelock College, where she has coordinated the child life and family center care program in the graduate school for several years. She also teaches a summer program in London, in which students gain experience in health care and hospital settings.

Marcia began her career as a nurse working with maternal and child health care in pediatrics and obstetrics. In these settings, she developed an appreciation of the role of play from infancy through childhood. She taught nursing in higher education, and then returned to get a degree in early childhood and child life in order to better understand child development.

Marcia is a strong advocate of play and its value in making health care environments a positive place for children and their families. Marcia lives in Wayland, Massachusetts. Her growing brood of grandchildren continues to teach her about the importance of play.

Fran Henderson is working with preschool-age children as a special education teacher at a non-public school located in Hemet, California. She received a B.A. in human development with a specialization in early childhood education from Pacific Oaks College, where she also took the classes leading to her ECSE (Early Childhood Special Education) credential.

Fran met Betty Jones while studying at Pacific Oaks; their chapter in this volume resulted from their dialogue about children's play in an online independent study program.

Fran has a special interest in supporting children with special needs as they acquire the skills needed to participate in quality play. She has found that improving communication skills, including providing augmentative communication systems, is a wonderful starting point. Her future plans include returning to Pacific Oaks to complete her M.A. in human development. Fran lives in Hemet, California. She is pictured with Cody LaMon.

Elizabeth (Betty) Jones is a member of the faculty in human development at Pacific Oaks College and the codirector of its distance learning program. Betty has been instrumental in implementing online courses at Pacific Oaks for over seven years. Her chapter in this volume is based on an online independent study dialogue that she held with one of her students, Fran Henderson.

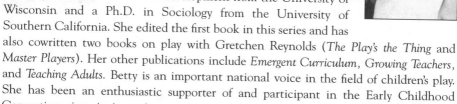

Betty has an M.A. in child development from the University of Wisconsin and a Ph.D. in Sociology from the University of Southern California. She edited the first book in this series and has also cowritten two books on play with Gretchen Reynolds (*The Play's the Thing* and *Master Players*). Her other publications include *Emergent Curriculum, Growing Teachers,* and *Teaching Adults.* Betty is an important national voice in the field of children's play. She has been an enthusiastic supporter of and participant in the Early Childhood Consortium since its inception.

Pacific Oaks College recently opened the Jones/Prescott Institute in honor of Betty's longtime commitment to children and the preparation of the adults who teach them. The institute serves as the community outreach arm of Pacific Oaks, through which a broad range of people and organizations can access the college. The institute promotes collaboration as well as constructivist and progressive education. Betty lives in California.

Amelia Klein, Ed.D., is an associate professor of early childhood education at Wheelock College. She has taught and supervised undergraduate students in preschool and primary settings. Her roots as an early childhood educator were established with over fifteen years in Head Start, kindergarten, and primary classrooms.

Amelia serves on the executive board of WACRA (World Association for Case Method Research and Application), an interdisciplinary international organization that is committed to interactive teaching. She has explored the topics of case methodology and teacher education in numerous publications.

Amelia founded the Native American Interest Group at Wheelock College, a voluntary group that seeks to inform and enlighten the college community about the past and present Native American reality in the United States. She came to know Carol Mills, her collaborator for this book, through that effort. Amelia lives in Needham, Massachusetts.

Diane Levin, Ph.D., is a professor of education at Wheelock College, where she teaches courses on children's play, violence prevention, and media literacy. She has an M.S. from Wheelock College and a Ph.D. from Tufts University.

Diane is an internationally known expert on how violence in media culture and society affects children's development and play. She is the author of six books, including *Before Push Comes to Shove: Building Conflict Resolution Skills with Children*; *Who's Calling the Shots? How to Respond Effectively to Children's Fascination with War Play, War Toys and Violent TV*; and *The War Play Dilemma*.

Diane consults around the world on media, violence, and play issues, and for U.S. organizations such as the American Psychological Association, the National Association for the Education for Young Children, National Public Television, Educators for Social Responsibility, and the Massachusetts Violence Prevention Task Force. Diane testified at the U.S. Senate Commerce Committee Hearings on the "Marketing of Violence to Children" and is a founder of the advocacy group TRUCE (Teachers Resisting Unhealthy Children's Entertainment). She lives in Cambridge, Massachusetts.

Karol Lunn, M.Ed. (deceased), received her a master's degree in Early Childhood from Wheelock College. She was a math resource teacher for the primary grades in the Wrentham, Massachusetts, school district, where she developed a mentoring support system for new teachers. She also worked in the Attleboro and Plainville, Massachusetts, schools and taught in both preschool and primary classrooms.

Karol devoted much of her career to working on behalf of young children in both public and private care and education settings. Karol lived in Massachusetts.

Shirley Malone-Fenner, Ph.D., is an associate professor of Psychology and Human Development at Wheelock College, where she teaches graduate and undergraduate courses in human development, counseling psychology, and family diversity. She also teaches a clinical course on violence in the lives of children and families, based on her extensive clinical experience with children and families.

Shirley is the founder of Wheelock's off-campus master's program in South Carolina, which is beginning its third cohort. She is also the director of the graduate Urban Teachers' Program.

Shirley is an advocate for equity and social justice in the professional preparation of educators. Her research interests include violence in the lives of children, case methodology in teaching practice, and urban schooling.

Joan Brooks McLane has a Ph.D. in educational psychology/child development from Northwestern University and an M.Ed. in child development from the Erikson Institute. Since 1979, she has been on the faculty of the Erikson Institute, where she teaches courses in cognitive development and play theory and practice. Before that, she taught in child care and elementary school.

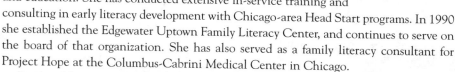

Joan's interests include early literacy development, family literacy, cognitive development, writing, and the role of play in development and education. She has conducted extensive in-service training and consulting in early literacy development with Chicago-area Head Start programs. In 1990 she established the Edgewater Uptown Family Literacy Center, and continues to serve on the board of that organization. She has also served as a family literacy consultant for Project Hope at the Columbus-Cabrini Medical Center in Chicago.

Joan's publications include a chapter in the second book of this series and several works on literacy development, family literacy, and cognitive development. Joan lives in Chicago.

Carol Mills, a member of the Ojibway Nation, has been active in the Indian education community for the past twenty years. She holds a master's degree in early childhood from Wheelock College.

Carol's recent consulting projects have included work with the American Indian Program Branch of the Head Start Program through the Head Start Bureau in Washington, D.C. In Boston, she assists the New England Aquarium with cultural programming. In Mashpee, Massachusetts, Carol has helped coordinate the community partnership grant for preschool children. Her most recent project is advising the Children's Museum in Boston about building a Wampanoag Web site.

Carol is the proud mother of four children and enjoys traveling to powwows to dance with her family. She lives in Mashpee, Massachusetts.

Amy Phillips, Ph.D., is an associate professor of education at Wheelock College and the coordinator of the interprofessional training program for undergraduate students. Her accomplishments include working with a group of educators from the Boston public schools to develop three new early education centers that have child-, family-, and community-friendly play spaces.

Amy was the editor of the second book in this series, and has also authored a chapter on "Instructional Principles for Creative Children with Learning Disabilities" for *Teaching Creative Children, K–8.*

Amy has worked extensively with children with autism as an art educator and play therapist. She is working on a book based on her experiences with children with autism and their families. Amy lives in Cambridge, Massachusetts.

Gretchen Reynolds has worked in early childhood and teacher education for many years. Her degrees include a Ph.D. in education from Claremont Graduate University and an M.S. in education from Bank Street College of Education. She is on the faculty of Algonquin College in Ottawa.

Gretchen is the coauthor of two volumes on the roles of teachers in supporting young children's masterful play. She is considered to be an important national and international voice in the field of children's play. Gretchen lives in Ottawa, Ontario, Canada.

Julie Spielberger is a senior research associate at the Chapin Hall Center for Children at the University of Chicago. She holds a Ph.D. in child development from the Erikson Institute and an M.S.T. in early childhood education from the University of Chicago. Before joining Chapin Hall, she worked extensively in training Head Start teachers and as a researcher and consultant with Head Start family literacy programs. She has also been an adjunct course instructor for Harold Washington College, Loyola University, and the Erikson Institute.

Julie is doing research on children's literacy development in after-school programs. She is involved in a national evaluation of an initiative to strengthen youth leadership, services, and community partnerships in public libraries in low-income areas. She has also managed consumer research for Playskool Toys, Inc. Her research interests include emergent literacy and the role of play in children's learning and development.

Julie came to know her coauthor, Joan McLane, while doing graduate study at the Erikson Institute. She lives in Chicago.

Kimberly P. Williams, Ph.D., is a researcher in learning sciences at the school of education and social policy at Northwestern University. She wrote her chapter for this book while she was a faculty member of the Erikson Institute.

Kimberly's current research addresses the use of a technology-integrated progressive science curriculum to support literacy. The role of literacy and language also continues to be a research interest.

Kimberly's published works include a cowritten article entitled "African-American Parents' Orientation toward Schools: The Implications of Social Class and School Characteristics." Kimberly lives in Evanston, Illinois.

Index

A

acculturation
  affects on people of color, 102–103
adult perceptions of culture
  affects on children's play, 57–58
African-Americans
  views on play, 74–75, 80–84
Allen, B, 123–130
anti-bias curriculum, 54, 57, 60–63
anti-bias teacher training, 54–55, 61–63
Ardley, J, 35–45
autism
  and communication systems, 124, 129
  and self-stimulation (stimming), 116–117, 137
  and teacher-child interactions, 116–121
  play in children with, 115–121, 137–138

B

Bartolini, V, 13–14, 17–19
Bateson, G, 115
Berk, L, 17, 18, 98, 142
Bernhard, J, 87
bicultural development, 100–103
Billman, J, 60
the bone game (Inuit game), 90–91
books (children's)
  and negative stereotypes, 58–59
Bowlby, J, 110
Bredekamp, S, 87–88
Brown, C, 115–116, 123–130, 134

C

Carlsson-Paige, N, 27, 31
Carter, M, 61
case methodology, x–xii, 51–52
case studies
  how to use (see case methodology)
child life specialists
  and preparation for medical procedures, 107–112
  different roles of, 111–112
children with special needs
  and goals for play, 137–140
  and play environments, 145
  facilitating play with, 124, 126–130
  supporting the play of, 133–146

cognitive development
  and play, 52, 83–84, 98–99, 134, 136
cognitive dissonance, 60–61
community
  and self-identity, 101
conflict resolution
  and play, 21–28
conflict resolution skills, 27–28
Cooper, R, 52
Copple, C, 87–88
Cornelius, C, 60
Cortés, C, 58
creative play
  vs. imitative play, 21, 27
cultural curriculum
  development of, 97–98, 100–102
cultural democracy (theory), 102
cultural immersion
  and bicultural development, 100–103
  and the development of community, 95–97, 100–103
  in preschool programs, 88–97, 100–103
cultural knowledge (dominant culture)
  sources of, 57–59
cultural learning
  and play, 52, 61–63
cultural meanings of play, 62–63, 73–75, 80–84
cultural myopia, 74
cultural sensitivity in teachers, 51–52
culturally appropriate practice, 53–55, 62–63, 97–98
culture, 74
  child's, and affects on play, 31, 62–63
Curtis, D, 61

D

Darder, A, 102
DeGaetano, Y, 60
Derman-Sparks, L, 60, 97, 101–102
developmentally appropriate practice, 14, 55, 60
developmentally delayed children
  play in, 136–137, 145–146
diversity
  children's concepts of, 57–60
  teacher education and, 87, 103
  teaching of, 54, 59–63
Dowd, F, 58

E

emergent curriculum,
  and children with special needs, 140–146
Ericson, L, 35–45

F

Fung, H, 81–82

G

Galda, L, 9
Gardner, H, 17
Goleman, D, 17, 18
Grandin, T, 120
Greenberg, P, 61

H

Hall, N, 60
Hartley, M, 107–112
Henderson, F, 133–146
Hernandez, H, 60
Hesse, P, 58
hostile reciprocity
  in children's play, 91–92
Hyun, E, 61

I

imitative play
  and affects on development and learning, 21
  and media-linked toys, 21
  and problem-solving skills, 21–22, 26–27
  vs. creative play, 21
inclusive preschool programs, 13–14
Indians. See Native Americans
individual educational plans (IEPs), 134,
  138–139, 142
interpersonal conflict
  and skill development, 44
Inuit culture
  and preschool education, 88–97, 99–103

J

Johanessen, L, 66
Jones, E, 5, 88, 98, 99, 102, 136, 133–146

K

Kingson, J, 107, 111
Klein, A, 35, 51–55, 57–62
Klugman, E, 52
knowledge construction
  and play, 3, 5, 21
Kritchevsky, S, 145
K-W-L (Know-Wonder-Learn), 61

L

Lakin, M, 88
Lee, E, 60
Levin, D, 21–28, 31, 52
Levine, R, 80
Loranger, N, 107
Lunn, K, 14–17

M

Malaguzzi, L, 98
Malone-Fenner, S, 65–69
Mann, J, 36
Marchant, C, 115–116, 123, 134
master play, 98, 136–137
McLane, J, 3–11, 52
media
  and cultural stereotypes, 58
  and imitative play, 21
medical procedures
  child life specialists and, 107–112
  preparation for, and parents' role, 107–112
  preparation for, and play, 108–112
Meier, T, 52, 73–74, 99, 115, 121
Mills, C, 55–57, 62–63
modeling behavior (teacher to child), 15–18
Morrow, L, 9
multicultural education
  and early childhood practice, 59–62
  for teachers, 54–55
multiple intelligences, 17
Murrell, P, 52, 73–74, 99, 115, 121

N

Native Americans
  in contemporary society, 54–57, 59
  perceptions of, in children's play, 51–55
  portrayals of, in classrooms, 51–55
  sources of information about, 61
  stereotypes about, in education and society,
    54–59
  traditional understandings of play, 62–63
Nimmo, J, 88, 144

O

Oldsen, G, 35
opportunity education, 81–82

P

parent-child play, 74–84. See also teacher-child
  play
parent-teacher communication
  and cultural differences, 73–75, 81–84
Pellegrini, A, 9
Peters, E, 101

Phillips, A, 115–122
Phillips, C, 101, 102–103
Piaget, J, 99
play
    and adult roles, 3–11, 15–19, 21–22. *See also* teacher-child play; parent-child play
    and conflict resolution, 21–28
    and emergent literacy, 9
    and inappropriate behavior, 13–19
    and knowledge construction, 3, 5, 21, 98,102
    and multicultural issues, 51–55, 59–63
    and the development of community, 88
    and the development of cultural knowledge, 3, 51–55, 59–60, 62–63, 87–103
    and the development of problem-solving skills, 3, 21–28
    and social skill development, 15–19, 21–28, 44–45, 83–84, 123–130
    as a context for learning, 4
    as a medium for cultural learning, 52, 59, 62, 87–88, 95, 98–103
    cultural meanings of, 31, 62–63, 73–84
    development of community and, 88
    impact on development and learning, 9, 13, 102
    meaning of, for young children, 52
    perceptions of, by college students, 52, 55
    racism in, 65–69
play-based curriculum, 126, 129–130
play-deprived children, 26–27
play entry, 14–19, 38, 41–42
play materials
    as resources for learning, 59
Poklemba, D, 58
Prescott, E, 91
pretend play, 3–11, 52, 77–80, 82–84, 98
    and cultural learning, 88, 98–99
    as a symbol system, 98–99
    See also sociodramatic play
the prison game (children's game), 66–68
professional development, x, 35–37, 44–45, 66
    and multicultural education, 60–63

Q
Quakers
    theories on play and behavior, 37, 43–45

R
racial identity, 100–103
    and play, 68–69, 102–103
racially segregated preschool programs. *See* cultural immersion
racism
    and bicultural development, 102–103

and education, 57–63
    in children's play, 65–69
Ramsey, P, 57, 61, 97–98
representational play, 17
Reynolds, G, 5, 87–103, 136, 138,139
Robertson, J, 110
Rudney, G, 35

S
scaffolding, 5, 18, 87–88, 135–136, 141, 142
Schrader, C, 9
Seale, D, 58
Seefeldt, C, 57, 60
Shelton, T, 112
Slapin, B, 58
social environment
    and formation of negative stereotypes, 59
social skills
    development of, and play, 15–19, 21–28, 83–84, 123–130
sociocultural theory of learning (Vygotsky), 98
sociodramatic play, 51. *See also* pretend play
    and cultural learning, 59, 88
Spielberger, J, 3–11, 52
Stepanak, J, 112
stereotypes
    affect on development of self, 58
    in play, 65–69
superhero play, 22–23, 30–31, 38–39
symbolic play
    and early literacy acquisition, 9

T
teacher-child play, 117–118. *See also* parent-child play
tourist curriculum, 97
Tungasuvvingat Inuit Head Start Program, 88–97, 99–101

V
violence and aggression in play, 26–28, 30–31, 36–45
Vygotsky, L, 8, 17, 65, 82, 98–99

W
Williams, D, 120
Williams, K, 73–84
Winsler, A, 98

Z
zone of proximal development, 8–9, 65, 142

Other Resources from Redleaf Press

Theories of Childhood: An Introduction to Dewey, Montessori, Erikson, Piaget, and Vygotsky
by Carol Garhart Mooney
Theories of Childhood examines the work of five groundbreaking educational theorists in relation to early education. Each theorist's ideas are presented to help teachers and students look to the foundations of child care for solutions and guidance in classrooms today.

The Art of Awareness: How Observation Can Transform Your Teaching
by Deb Curtis and Margie Carter
Do more than watch children—*be* with children. Covering different aspects of children's lives and how to observe them, as well as tips for gathering and preparing documentation, *The Art of Awareness* is an inspiring look at how to see the children in your care—and how to see what they see.

Reflecting Children's Lives: A Handbook for Planning Child-Centered Curriculum
by Deb Curtis and Margie Carter
Keep children and childhood at the center of your curriculum and rethink ideas about scheduling, observation, play, materials, space, and emergent themes with these original approaches.

Children at the Center: Reflective Teachers at Work (Video)
by Margie Carter
Follow teachers in two programs as they redesign their classrooms and evaluate their roles for a child-centered curriculum. This video explores exciting approaches to setup, scheduling, and curriculum planning.

Setting Sail: An Emergent Curriculum Project (Video)
by Deb Curtis and Margie Carter
See how a child's interest in a song about the *Titanic* grows into an exciting classroom project. This video examines how teachers foster artistic expression, scientific knowledge, language development, and social skills through this project.

Thinking Big: Extending Emergent Curriculum Projects (Video)
by Margie Carter, Sarah Felstiner, and Ann Pelo
See how teachers discover emergent curriculum themes in children's play and extend them into in-depth project work.

800-423-8309
www.redleafpress.org

8741